739.27

HARROW
LODGE

130019

JEWELLERY

MAKERS

•

MOTIFS

•

HISTORY

•

TECHNIQUES

JEWELLERY

MAKERS

•

MOTIFS

•

HISTORY

•

TECHNIQUES

DIANA SCARISBRICK · JACK OGDEN · RONALD LIGHTBOWN
PETER HINKS · PATRICIA BAYER · VIVIENNE BECKER · HELEN CRAVEN

THAMES AND HUDSON

A QUARTO BOOK

First published in Great Britain in 1989 by
Thames and Hudson Limited, London

Copyright © 1989 Quarto Publishing plc

All rights reserved

This book was designed and produced by
Quarto Publishing plc
The Old Brewery
6 Blundell Street
London N7 9BH

Consultant editor Diana Scarisbrick

Project editor Henrietta Wilkinson
Editor Mary Chesshyre
Designer Hazel Edington
Picture researcher Deirdre O'Day

Editorial director Carolyn King
Art director Moira Clinch

Typeset in Great Britain by Pearl Graphics, London
Ampersand, Bournemouth and QV Typesetting

Manufactured in Hong Kong by Regent Publishing Services Ltd
Printed by Leefung-Asco Printers Ltd, Hong Kong

CONTENTS

INTRODUCTION

The ancient goldsmith's mastery of the techniques of enamelling and filigree is demonstrated in this detail from a gold jewel for the forehead. The crescent, which hangs from a round disc, terminates in rosettes at each end, and from it hang smaller rosettes and plaited gold chains. The enamelled gold honeysuckle in the centre is a classical motif often executed in diamonds by jewellers of the late 19th and early 20th century.

The story of jewellery over seven thousand years of civilization covers the response of successive generations of craftsmen and women to the challenge of fashioning rare and precious materials into personal ornaments which express the prevailing artistic style.

This rich and diverse panorama begins in the ancient world, when the basic techniques of the goldsmith were mastered at an astonishingly early date. Outstanding achievements came from the Etruscans who brought filigree and granulation techniques to a peak of perfection never since equalled, and from the Hellenistic court jewellers who mastered the art of modelling human figures for earrings, necklaces and bracelets bright with red garnets and enamel. Sometimes there were marked changes of style: the luxurious Roman gold ornaments laden with green emeralds and shining white pearls contrast sharply with the barbaric, powerful polychrome jewels of the Dark Ages which followed the end of the Empire.

An entirely new note was struck in the Middle Ages when jewels expressed the ideals of Christianity and chivalry in the language of the cathedral builders with crockets and canopied niches. Another high point was attained in the classical climate of the Renaissance when goldsmiths created historiated compositions highlighted with enamels and gemstones. This figurative style vanished in the next phase, when the reign of the gem-setter began and the contribution of the goldsmith declined progressively as jewels became no more than a vehicle for the display of gemstones and artistry was subordinated to a concern with intrinsic value. In the rococo period the trend toward lightness and asymmetry resulted in less dense and more open designs which adapted elegantly to the severe outlines of the Neo-classical style current from the 1770s.

A Taste for Opulence

The complex course of 19th-century developments begins with the grandiose jewels that were created for the court of the Emperor Napoleon and which set the standard for the rest of Europe long after the defeat at Waterloo in 1815. At the same time emerged Romanticism, a movement inspired by nostalgia for the picturesque world of the Middle Ages and Renaissance. Around

1850, Romanticism merged with a strong current of revivalism embracing the whole of history and leading to the recreation of the gold ornaments of antiquity and the Dark Ages for daytime wear. The growing taste for luxury, encouraged by prosperity, low taxation and a hierarchical social system, was expressed by increasingly opulent displays of diamonds after the discovery of mines in South Africa in the 1860s. This event transformed the character of jewellery which for several decades concentrated on glitter and sparkle rather than on colour, design and the expression of ideas. At the turn of the century, however, there was a two-fold reaction against the banality of so much diamond jewellery. First Cartier and Boucheron adopted a new style, of 18th-century inspiration, comprising trelliswork and garlands of stylized flowers, using platinum for settings. This diamond jewellery epitomizes the gracious elegance of the Belle Epoque.

At around the same time, the Art Nouveau jewellers, led by René Lalique, created a great stir at the Paris Exhibition of 1900 with designs taken directly from nature and executed in materials such as horn and ivory, chosen for their aesthetic quality rather than intrinsic value. Although beautiful as works of art, they were not suited for practical purposes and the style disappeared – as did the garland style – with the outbreak of the First World War. Soon after the peace of 1918 came jewels in the Art Deco style, which owed nothing to tradition, and little to nature, but instead was closely associated with contemporary art – Cubism and Abstractionism – and the streamlined architecture of the Bauhaus, softening only in the mid-1930s when figurative and floral motifs were re-introduced by Cartier.

Fine jewellery after the Second World War was adapted to the taste of a clientele buying for investment as well as for show. The emphasis was on the quality of the stones, perfectly faceted, and mounted in streamlined flexible settings in tune with current couture fashion. Simultaneously, all over the world, artist jewellers were emerging both for the design and execution of jewels, often selling direct to clients. This movement, which stems from the 19th-century Arts and Crafts tradition, has recently been affected by the high cost of precious stones and metal, leading to experiments with cheap materials such as plastic.

The Virgin and Child, favourite theme of medieval sculpture was also interpreted by jewellers in gold, enamelled in the round. This group probably came from a morse, or large brooch designed to fasten a priest's chasuble when officiating at the altar.

INTRODUCTION

A love of flowers and leaves has inspired jewellers throughout history. Mid-19th century taste demanded botanical jewels glittering with diamonds and large in scale as this bouquet of carnations and roses. Some of the flowers are mounted on trembler springs for additional glitter.

The Supremacy of the Parisian Jewellers

Amid so much diversity some factors have remained constant for long periods, notably the supremacy of Paris. Since 1200–1400, when the Parisian jewellers were regarded as pre-eminent in design and craftsmanship, this lead has, for the most part, been maintained. French designs were diffused abroad in engraved editions of pattern books published from the 16th to the 19th centuries, while practical expertise emigrated with Huguenot craftsmen after the Revocation of the Edict of Nantes in 1685. Others were invited to work at the courts of foreign rulers, and visiting ladies took advantage of their time in Paris to have their jewels reset. Although the French Revolution of 1789 brought this luxury trade to a standstill, it was triumphantly revived under Napoleon. Even the collapse of the Second Empire in 1870 could not shake it. The great dynasties of Cartier, Boucheron and Chaumet survived the disaster unscathed and expanded their empires into the 20th century, setting up branches in London, New York, Switzerland and Japan. It was from Paris, too, that the pioneers of Art Nouveau and Art Deco emerged to generate the ideas which the great jewellers then transformed into fashionable jewels. As a result of the close connection between the leading jewellers and couture houses, designs have been conceived in harmony with the latest fashions in dress; this has contributed to the continuing success of the French firms in the post-Second World War period.

Whereas some motifs, like snakes, only appear intermittently in the long history of jewellery, others have been continually reinterpreted. The flowers and leaves ornamenting Hellenistic diadems also decorate the shoulders of medieval rings, are enamelled on the covers of 17th-century lockets and watch-cases, and, studded with diamonds and coloured stones, appear as asymmetrical bouquets for the 18th-century lady to pin in her hair or on her bodice. At the 1878 International Exhibition, the stand of the Parisian jeweller, O. Massin, attracted great crowds who came to stare at his diamond botanical jewellery, which, mounted on trembler springs, captured the grace and lightness of the living flower. One of the great achievements of 20th-century jewellery has been the interpretation of floral designs in the exacting "invisible set-ting" technique introduced by Van Cleef & Arpels in 1936.

Jewels as Love Tokens

Jewels are the most prized of all love tokens, and motifs expressing sentiment have a long history: hands clasped in trust, Cupid's arrows, gimmel rings with twin hoops and bezels symbolic of the married state, lockets containing the hair and miniatures of loved ones. Whereas these are not acceptable to 20th-century taste, the heart, which first appears in medieval jewellery, and then – jewelled or enamelled, single, twinned, wounded, flying or crowned–in all successive periods, maintains its appeal today.

Cameos and intaglios have also seen successive revivals. In antiquity they were valued above all other precious objects, and those that descended to medieval princes were likewise mounted in richly jewelled settings of which the Schaffhausen Onyx is the most celebrated. The difficult art of gem engraving was practised again in the Renaissance when hat badges, pendants, necklaces, rings and bracelets were set with cameos and intaglios representing mythological divinities, the heroes of classical history, and ancient and modern illustrious men and women. In the 18th century Madame de Pompadour – herself a gifted engraver – brought engraved hardstones back into fashion for jewellery, and demand in the Neo-classical period was so great that it could only be met by Josiah Wedgwood's ceramic reproductions. Throughout the 19th century, cameos were a favourite form of daytime jewel, signifying both high culture and the experience of travel, for the best source was the workshops of Rome, heirs to a tradition going back to the Roman Empire.

Unlike their settings, engraved hardstones have escaped the fate of recycling, and so it is possible to follow the development of this art throughout its history. This is not the case with jewellery, which is almost always doomed as it passes from one generation to the next for resetting according to the latest fashion. Thus, what has come down to us only represents a small part of a much wider picture, and the objects illustrated in this book provide only a hint of the glorious creations of the jewellers of past times.

The supremacy of the French jeweller which began in the early 13th century has been maintained ever since with the exception of a few brief periods. Talent may pass down through several generations, as in the firm of Boucheron, who made these striking jade, onyx and diamond earrings, c. 1924 . Founded in 1858 it is at the centre of an empire which now extends to Japan.

Bracelets and other ornaments with animal motifs. Part of a large hoard of goldwork with the so-called Oxus treasure, from the 5th-3rd centuries BC, found over one hundred years ago in Afghanistan.

CHAPTER ONE

THE ANCIENT WORLD

Cast and hammered gold

·

Egypt and Mesopotamia

·

Greeks and Romans

·

The influence of Christendom

·

The Dark Ages

JACK OGDEN

INTRODUCTION

Lapis lazuli and carnelian are combined with gold (and a little silver) in these Sumerian ornaments from Ur which date from around 2500 BC. These were the favourite stones in early Near Eastern jewellery. The simple but strong shapes of the beads and earrings alongside the stylized gold flower-heads and leaves, accent the timeless majesty of these early court jewels.

The Age of Gold was a legendary, Utopian period early in man's history. It is aptly described. Gold occurs naturally in the earth in an attractive ready-to-use state, and so was one of the first metals ever used. The softness of gold meant that it had a greater ornamental than functional value; it was the colour of the sun; and it was not affected by corrosion and decay. The beauty of gold, in the eyes of early man, meant that it was frequently singled out as a fitting gift for the gods or a suitable accompaniment for the dead. Its unalterability, in chemical terms, supported such human desires and ensured that gold artefacts from the earliest periods could survive in near pristine condition.

The concept of jewellery is timeless. People have always had an instinctive desire to adorn themselves. Simple ornaments of berries, soft stones, animal teeth and the like date back to the Stone Age, as do some simple gold objects. However, the construction of jewellery from gold or silver, and the combination of these with coloured stones, really began in earnest around the beginning of the Bronze Age. So, in the ancient Near East, gold and coloured-stone jewellery is rare in burials much before about 3000 BC; In Western Europe, a gold jewellery industry was flourishing soon after 2500 BC.

The Old World has thus seen a production of gold jewellery for some 5000 years with a continuous development in designs and techniques. Designs reflect all aspects of the societies in which they blossomed. Religion, superstition, social organization, economics, trade, and warfare all played a part. As new techniques were introduced, new decorative ideas were possible and new materials, such as harder stones or coloured glasses and enamel, could be incorporated.

Gold can easily be hammered out into thin sheets, so ancient gold jewellery was usually made from thin sheet gold. Cast gold ornaments were unusual except in certain regions, such as Western Europe. Ancient gold was made with a minimum assortment of tools and these were simply made from metal, wood or bone.

By about 2000 BC, the goldsmiths in the Near East had developed the skills necessary to form, manipulate and join very small components. The ultimate expression of this skill was the technique of granulation, which spread rapidly through the Eastern Mediterranean and the Near East. Granulation work consists of designs of minute gold spheres each of which can be well under .5mm (.02 in) in diameter. Much of the earliest wire filigree and granulation work is, however, not particularly fine, which can give a somewhat barbaric appearance to the jewellery.

The combination of coloured stones with gold was popular in Egypt and Mesopotamia from an early period. Cornelian and lapis lazuli were the favourites, but green feldspar and other stones were also employed. In Europe the fashion seems to have been for gold alone and here

coloured stones were seldom set in gold much before the Roman period.

Extensive trade contacts meant that there was a general constancy in the techniques and materials used in jewellery making throughout the Near East. With jewellery designs, however, more localized characteristics are identifiable. In most parts of the Old World, the designs are essentially abstract, geometric or organic in form. We find spirals, circles, rosettes, and fruit-like fluted beads, timeless forms that can be paralleled in most parts of the world and

in all periods. The only civilization that stands out in contrast is Egypt: strongly representational forms were very much a characteristic of Egyptian jewellery, which could quite literally spell out meanings in its designs. In most other parts of the Old World, from Ireland to Persia, such obviously representational designs were for long the exception rather than the rule. We can think of much Egyptian jewellery as icons in which coloured stones take the place of pigment and such frippery as granulation work is rarely found. This representational approach has its parallel in the strictly defined pictorial hieroglyphics of written Egyptian, which contrasts with, say, the abstract, wedge-like cuneiform writing of Mesopotamia.

In the gold jewellery produced by the Minoan and Mycenaean civilizations in Greece, Crete and Cyprus the emphasis is again on goldwork rather than stones, though rudimentary enamelwork is found – perhaps its earliest occurrence in the world. Egyptian influence in some Mycenaean jewellery is obvious, but there are also links with Western Asia and Northern Europe. The Mycenaeans wore gold seal rings and earrings. Signet rings had been known in Egypt since around 2000 BC, but were never a characteristic of Western Asia, whereas the Egyptians, for some unfathomable reason, did not wear earrings prior to about 1500 BC, one thousand years after their Mesopotamian counterparts had first worn them. Egyptian rings were initially seals – usually the seal took the form of an oval representation of the scarab beetle, the flat base of which was engraved with a design that could be used to make seal impressions. In Western Asia the traditional seal type was an engraved cylinder that could be rolled over clay to leave an impression. Such seals were not well suited to setting in rings but were better worn as pendants.

The Iron Age

Soon after 1000 BC we see a wind of change in jewellery designs, except in Egypt with its all-pervading conservatism. The new styles came from and were spread by the Phoenicians, while the increase in the degree of precision and repetition of techniques might well reflect the new availability of iron tools. It is somewhat ironic that the Phoenician style was, ultimately, Egyptian in origin, but, newly interpreted and with an accent on granulation and other fine decorative techniques, it spread round the Mediterranean from Syria to Spain. The superb, delicate jewellery of the Etruscans, for example, best known for its minuscule and perfect granulation work, owes much of its inspiration to the Phoenicians and is very closely related in technical terms.

As the Phoenicians travelled the Mediterranean world, other influences were having an effect to the east and north. Animal motifs, perhaps originating in the southern steppes of Russia, spread down into Turkey and Persia and emerged in ornaments such as bracelets and torques with animal-head terminals. As the Persian Empire grew, a variety of motifs, styles, techniques and even craftsmen intermixed over a vast region. Further west the Celtic floral and animal styles appeared, perhaps filtering across from the same Russian steppes. The Celtic forms, to which Art Nouveau would look more than 2000 years later, give a contradictory feeling of freedom combined with a sense of mysterious secrecy. This European Celtic style passed into

As the Roman period progressed, men often aspired to wear as many gold rings as their fingers and purses could bear. The rise of a large middle class with access to gold (in the form of coins) greatly widened the market for jewellery. The ring shown here has a gold bezel delicately chiselled with a figure of the goddess Roma being offered a victor's wreath by a small winged Victory. The inscription tells us that the original owner was called Gerontius. This ring was found with other jewellery at Tarsus in Syria and dates to around AD 300.

Anglo-Saxon, Viking and other Dark Ages jewellery.

As the Persian Empire gradually fell to Alexander the Great from 334 BC, the homogenization of Near Eastern jewellery became almost complete. Even in conservative Egypt, Hellenism prevailed: initially the Egyptian and Greek traditions in jewellery co-existed, but then the age-old Egyptian forms were superseded almost entirely by cosmopolitan Hellenistic styles.

Greek jewellery of this period is characterized by its abundant applied decoration, most typically fine filigree arranged in the form of spirals, waves and floral sprays. It is less self-absorbed in intricacy than Etruscan work and granulation was mainly employed to highlight or punctuate the filigree work. The filigree itself was very frequently embellished with enamel, but unfortunately the ravages of time have meant that Hellenistic jewellery is seldom seen today in its full polychrome splendour. Blood-red garnets were the most popular stones in Hellenistic jewellery, though by the 2nd century BC emeralds, pearls and sometimes onyxes were also popular.

Gold jewellery set with coins became popular towards the end of the 3rd century AD. In many cases it would have been a gift — perhaps a betrothal exchange or a presentation from the Emperor to a favoured subject. This magnificent pendant of delicate chisel-pierced openwork is embellished with high busts of mythological figures and is set with a double-solidus minted in AD 321.

Rome, Byzantium and the West

In the Near East, particularly in Syria, the Hellenistic taste for effusive decoration continues into the early centuries of the Christian Era, but in Italy a more severe, Roman style of jewellery came into existence. Gone is the fiddly precision and fear of open spaces of Etruscan goldwork. In its place we have a love of stronger and starker forms such as the bracelets and earrings composed of simple burnished gold hemispheres. Where coloured stones are used pearls and emeralds reign supreme, not the bright red garnets and polychrome enamels of the Hellenistic world.

Paradoxical as it might seem, we have very little Roman jewellery from Italy, apart from the large quantity of ornaments from Pompeii and the neighbouring towns devastated by the eruption of Vesuvius in AD 79. Most surviving Roman-period jewellery appears elsewhere in the Roman Empire. Much is from Asia Minor, Syria and the Levant. This jewellery is supplemented by finds from Europe which establish the overall unity of Roman jewellery. As the Roman period progressed the trend was away from the starker Italian Roman forms and back towards the Hellenistic tradition with its love of ornamentation and coloured stones.

With the spread of christianity through the Roman Empire in the early 4th century AD Christian iconography superseded, or, in many cases, adapted, pagan Roman and Hellenistic designs. Coloured stones were popular, particularly emeralds, pearls and sapphires. When the real stones were not available glass substitutes were used – with or without the knowledge of the buyer. There was a love of intricate goldwork, particularly the pierced open-work that gives lace-like lattices of gold. Gold coins began to be worn set in rings and hanging from pendants. All this early Byzantine jewellery provided outward signs of wealth and affluence that appalled the early Christian Fathers.

Christianity itself added a new repertoire of motifs, but that did not mean the loss of earlier traditions. For example, when we see Byzantine rings with bezels in the form of lotus flowers – which had become a symbol of the Virgin Mary and Christ's birth – we are also looking at the age-old Egyptian symbol of the lotus as the birthplace of the young sun god.

History books usually tell us that with the demise of the Roman Empire Europe was plunged into the Dark Ages for half a millennium before re-emerging in the dawn of the Medieval period. The jewellery historian knows how untrue this is. Jewellery produced by the Saxons, Merovingians, Franks, Ostrogoths, Vikings and others compares favourably with anything produced before or since, both in terms of design and technical ability. The goldsmith's craft continued, without a harsh break, from the Ancient to the Medieval world, forever building on, and adapting, the designs and concepts of earlier jewellers.

A modern map indicating some of the major gold and gem sources of the ancient world. Different gemstones were favoured at different periods; for example, emeralds and pearls were only widely used from the Hellenistic period onwards, and sapphires were seldom worn before Roman times.

INFLUENCES

Following the adoption of the Christian faith by the Eastern Roman Empire in the early 4th century AD, jewellers and other artists adapted and combined both Christian and pre-Christian iconography. In many cases, iconographic continuation was possible by reinterpreting earlier concepts in Christian terms.

In Christian art the lily or lotus flower was a symbol of the Virgin Mary. This 7th century ring (**1**), has a bezel in the form of a lotus flower and its allusion to the Virgin Mary is strengthened by the pierced inscription on the shank by which the wearer appeals to the protection of the Theotokos (the Mother of God).

1

2

3

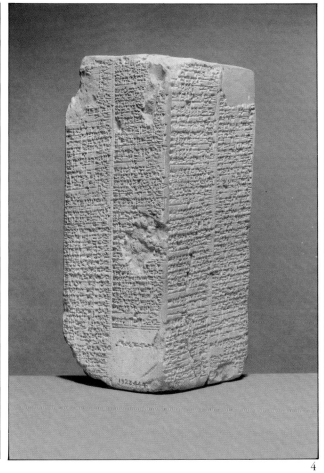

4

In Ancient Egyptian mythology the young sun god, Horus, came forth from the lotus flower. Looking at a lotus (**2**), which opens to the sun each morning, we can understand how such a legend began. In Egyptian art we often see representations of the young sun god appearing from a lotus. The pair of gold bracelets (**3**), dating from about 940 BC, show the birth of the sun god with flanking uraeus serpents — the protectors of royalty — a highly suitable design for the original wearer who was a son of a Pharaoh. The bracelets were inlaid with lapis lazuli and blue glass although much of the inlay is now missing.

The Egyptian hieroglyphic script shown (**5**) is from the temple of Kom Ombo. The necklet from the tomb of Tutankhamun (**6**) combines a variety of symbols. The main pendant shows the eye of Horus flanked by the Royal Protectors. The counterbalance is composed of two symbols, helping the general welfare of the wearer. Art was representational and thus could be "read"

5 6

In Egyptian art there was an overall unity of proportions and motifs whereas in Western Asia there was a less formal canon and art was thus not so obviously readable. The Sumerian necklet and ornamental disks from Ur (**7**) (c.2500 BC) cannot be compared with, or interpreted in comparison with, the wedge-like cuneiform writing seen here impressed into a Sumerian clay tablet (**4**). What we see as abstraction in both writing and jewellery designs must reflect something of the underlying society. This is also true of the formal pictorial nature of Egyptian writing and has a close connection to the set repertoire of Egyptian jewellery motifs.

7

GOLD IN THE BRONZE AGE

The use of shells, as in this 7000-year-old necklace from Arpachiya in what is now Iraq (**1**), dates back to time immemorial. The sliced cowrie shells were originally filled with a red substance which would have contrasted with the shiny black obsidian beads. Obsidian beads are hard to cut and polish and their maker saved time and effort by leaving the backs unpolished. The black bead, top centre, is of mud not obsidian. The original thread, which has since disappeared, would have been of organic fibre or, perhaps, animal hair.

Designs and concepts can often transcend the nature of the materials used. We can see this in the similar overall forms of the jet necklace from Scotland (**2**) and the gold collar from Ireland (**3**). Both date from around 1800–1500 BC and have strictly geometric ornamentation.

In keeping with its age and Western European origin, the gold collar is formed from a single piece of hammered gold sheet. The decoration is incised or scored, a process rarely seen in Eastern Mediterranean goldwork of the Bronze Age.

THE EARLY JEWELLERS

Our knowledge of the earliest jewellers is gleaned from pictorial and literary evidence. Reliefs in Egyptian tombs show all aspects of the craft from the basic recovery of the raw materials, through the working methods, to the finished articles being displayed, recorded and weighed. Texts refer to important men bearing a variety of titles connected with the supervision of the goldsmith's craft. The craftsmen under their control, depicted bent over their anvils or drilling stone beads, are anonymous.

A glimpse of the lives of the individual craftsmen is better obtained from the less formal texts of Western Asia. These include inventories listing all types of jewellery. We also learn about the administration of the workshops, the types of precious stones and their origins, the numbers of craftsmen, and,

A detail from a relief in the tomb of Mereruka at Saqqara, Egypt, showing two craftsmen with a newly made necklet, c. 2300 BC.

possibly we hear of itinerant craftsmen.

A recent, remarkable discovery at Larsa in Iraq was a sealed jar dating from 1738 BC, which contained jewellers' tools, weights, gold jewellery, lapis lazuli and other stones, scrap silver, and, most interestingly, a seal bearing the name of the original owner. The jar was found in what

had been his workshop. This is so far the only occurrence from the ancient world of evidence of a named jeweller, the site of his workshop, his tools and specimens of his handiwork.

The workshop of this named jeweller was situated in a temple and, indeed, most of the jewellers of which we have a record were connected with a temple or a

court. The circulation of gold, silver and valuable gemstones was for long controlled by temple or state.

Whether working for temple or for court, or plying his trade among the richer members of society, the ancient goldsmith used remarkably few and unsophisticated tools. Nevertheless, with skill and time at his disposal he was able to produce exquisite jewellery which has not only withstood the test of time but has also acted as an inspiration to jewellers in recent centuries.

The fine necklace (4) with its elaborate and precise granulation work was supposedly found at Dilbat in Iraq. On the basis of the technique used and the style of some of the elements, the necklet can be dated to c. 1700 BC. The pair of figures on the sides probably represent the goddess Lama.

The granulation work and the fluted sheet-gold beads have parallels in other gold jewellery from Iraq and Syria and show the high levels of workmanship, and basic homogeneity, of the jewellery of the period.

4

5

The geometric form of the gold pendant (5) contrasts with the representational nature of most jewellery from ancient Egypt. The pendant would have originally contained a charm of some sort. A date of c. 1900–1800 BC puts the fine granulation work amongst the earliest known from Egypt.

GOLD IN THE BRONZE AGE

1

2

3

The two pairs of earrings, pendant and necklace (**1**) were all excavated in 1896 at the site of Enkomi in Cyprus. They date from the Mycenaean period, around 1400–1300 BC.

The geographical position of the island of Cyprus laid it open to influences from Egypt, Western Asia and the Aegean. The goldwork shown here, however, is entirely Cypriot. The long, drop-hoop earrings of hollow sheet gold, and the ear hoops with embossed, highly stylized bull-head pendants, are most typically Cypro-Mycenaean. The necklet, composed of gold shield-like motifs, spheri-cal and spiral gold beads and carnelian beads, might harken back to foreign concepts, but it is a fine version of another favoured

Cypriot ornament.

The little gold sphere pendant represents a pomegranate and has a minute, repetitive triangle design in granulation.

The Egyptian scarab beetle, symbol of the sun and creation, was a popular motif. This winged scarab, inlaid with coloured stones and faience (**2**), dates from c. 1885 BC. The scarab clasps the

sun and, like so much Egyptian jewellery, the motifs shown spell out a name in hieroglyphs, in this case one name of King Sesostris II. The wing span is only 3.5 cm (1.5 in).

Scarabs were also mounted in rings, their bases engraved to be used as seals. The gold and green jasper example (**3**) dates from around 1500 BC.

Unlike the Egyptian scarab seal, the traditional cylinder shaped seal from Western Asia was usually too large to be worn set in a ring. The usual way of carrying a cylinder seal was as a pendant. The very fine lapis lazuli mounted in gold was excavated at Ur, in modern Iraq, on the skeleton of a obviously important man (**4**). He also had gold bracelets, a necklet and other jewellery, all dating from c. 2100 BC.

4

6

5

The earliest European jewellery was usually made from one piece of gold. For separate components, rivets or folds were used, not soldering. This was also almost universally true of bronze jewellery. The gold spiral jewellery from Hungary (**5**) of about 1000 BC illustrates this simple construction. The jewellery consists of gold sheet hammered into wires and coiled to form brooches, pendants and a pectoral or diadem.

Jewellery from Egypt and Western Asia stands out in contrast to this with its expert use of soldering to join separate and often minuscule components. The diadem with star and gazelle motifs (**6**), found in the Egyptian Delta, combines a simple design with delicate workmanship. The form is more Western Asiatic than Egyptian in style and might be an import. It dates from around 1650–1550 BC.

NEW THEMES

2

The early centuries of the first millennium BC saw the establishment of Phoenician traders and colonists throughout the Mediterranean. Phoenician jewellery is characterized by its precise granulation work and its visually strong design. The motifs used were often Egyptian in origin but the realization was Phoenician. The Phoenician bracelet (**1**) looks almost Art Deco whilst the repeated motif might derive from the Egyptian hieroglyph for "gold". The bracelet is from Sardinia and dates from the 7th-6th centuries BC.

The precision of even Phoenician goldwork was surpassed by the Etruscans in central Italy. The highly intricate, if not overcrowded, disk earring (**2**) is of about the same age as the Phoenician bracelet but the granulation and filigree are on a much smaller scale. Etruscan techniques and assembly methods, however, were based on Phoenician ones. For example, the corroded hinge pins of the Phoenician bracelet are of silver – a metal used for similar structural purposes in Etruscan goldwork.

1

3

4

5

The naturalistic jewellery styles that spread through the Middle East and Europe in the first millennium BC probably derived from the Russian steppes, the home of the gold stag (3). This stag, probably a shield ornament, combines various animal forms and dates from around 500 BC.

Interactions with Persian and Greek forms resulted in a less barbaric animal style. The magnificent armlet with griffin terminals (5), one of a pair from the so-called Oxus Treasure, dates from around 400 BC. It was originally all inlaid with stones.

The naturalistic designs of Celtic Europe can have for us an Art Nouveau appearance, as in the detail of a gold torc of the 1st century BC, from Broighter in Ireland (4).

AFTER ALEXANDER

1

The necklace shown above (**1**) dates to around 300 BC and is of a type popular in the Hellenistic world as established by the conquests of Alexander the Great. A strap-like band of several narrow chains joined side by side supports a fringe of small spearhead and rosette pendants. The terminals are enlivened with garnets. Necklets of this type were worn suspended by pins from shoulder to shoulder rather than around the neck.

Hellenistic jewellery was often decorated with enamel, usually blue and green, but much of this has decayed with time. The enamel was normally positioned in cells formed from wire. This is the case on the terminals flanking the gold and garnet Herakles knot centrepiece (**2**) of the 3rd century BC. The birds pendants on the earrings (**3**) consist of a gold framework dipped into white enamel. This dipped enamel technique seems to have been an Italian speciality of the 2nd to 1st centuries BC.

2

3

Jewellery from the Hellenistic period shows a growing love of coloured stones and a trend away from elaborate filigree. The earring or pendant (**5**) and the necklet (**4**) show these changes in taste. The earring, a superb version of the well-known disk and lunate type, was found in southern Russia and dates to the end of the 4th century BC. The decoration consists of fine applied filigree work and the only colour is provided by the enamel placed in the filigree cells. The necklet consists of gold wire links threaded through emerald beads. This type of stone and gold linking is typical of the second half of the Hellenistic period. The lion-head terminals have banded black and white glass collars and the centrepieces are set with emeralds and a garnet. This necklet, from Asia Minor, dates from c. 150–50 BC.

4

5

PAGANS AND CHRISTIANS

The elaborate gold collar of which a detail is shown here (1) comes from Sweden and dates from the 6th century AD. Nevertheless the technical and stylistic approach shown in the granulation and filigree links back through three millennia and to the Mediterranean and Middle East.

1

CONTRACTS

In the Roman period, as in earlier times, the evidence we have for the day-to-day trade of the goldsmith comes from pictorial and textual evidence. It seems possible that the introduction of precious metal coinage by about 600 BC helped the jeweller by providing a ready means by which the man in the street could obtain gold. Certainly in the Hellenistic and Roman periods there is far more evidence regarding the purchase of jewellery by ordinary people.

The dry sands of Egypt have allowed the survival of a vast number of papyrus documents which

A gold armlet in the form of a snake of the 1st century AD, probably from Egypt.

shed light on all aspects of life in Egypt in the Roman period. Amongst these documents are

several dealing with jewellery transactions. One of these relates to an order for a pair of gold coiled snake armlets to be made for a customer. The document records that money was given by the customer with which the goldsmith was to purchase the gold. Snake armlets of the type that the document is probably referring to can be seen worn in pairs on the upper arms of women in 1st-century AD funerary depictions, as here on the gilded mummy mask

Goldwork from Pompeii and the neighbouring towns destroyed by the eruption of Vesuvius in 79 AD reveals a rather stark geometric style. The dome bracelets (2) are a characteristic example.

Close links can be seen between some jewellery from Pompeii and that of the same period from Egypt. The magnificent gilded mummy covering (3) depicts snake armlets (as above), snake bracelets (maybe a funerary convention and not an everyday style), earrings, necklets and rings. The latter include a snake ring on the third finger of the right hand, the normal finger for such rings.

2

3

4

Both dome bracelets and the gilt mask date to the 1st century AD.

The more Hellenistic tastes of the eastern Roman and early Byzantine periods contrast with the plainer Pompeian and early Romano-Egyptian styles.

A fine chisel-pierced openwork technique, as seen in the 4th-century AD necklet element from Asia Minor (**4**), was most popular in the early Byzantine period. (This gold and garnet element was stolen in 1982 and has not been recovered.)

5

The hoop earrings with their finely linked chain drops and pearls (**5**) are a good example of the simpler designs of some Byzantine jewellery. These probably come from Egypt and can be dated to the 5th to 6th centuries AD. The small gold granules where the pendant rings join the hoops help strengthen the joint and are typical of the type.

THE DARK AGES

The goldwork of the so-called Dark Ages can be compared favourably with anything produced before or since. This is as true of technique as it is of style and design. This can be illustrated by taking, as an example, the jewellery produced by the Vikings.

The two pendants in the form of faces (*1*), of silver not gold, date from around 800–1000 AD. In technique they are most visually reminiscent of Phoenician work (particularly that from Spain) –

though the Phoenicians seemingly could not produce granulation in silver.

The gold strap end (*3*) also shows fine quality filigree and granulation work. This dates from about the ninth century AD and was found in Norway.

The gold disk (*2*) from Sweden is the largest Viking example of a type of pendant termed a bracteate. The centre shows a stylised human head and a horse and is based on a coin.

1

2

3

One of the characteristics of Post-Roman European jewellery is the use of cloisonné set stones, most usually thin, flat slivers of garnet. These can be seen in a

seventh century belt buckle from Aker in Norway (*4*) plated with gold and silver and decorated with niello work.

4

Animal motifs, less obvious in the buckle, are clearly seen in the silver bracelet from Sweden of the eleventh century (5). The plaited hoop is typical Viking.

Ring brooches were popular in the Roman period and typical of Medieval jewellery. The two Viking Period examples (6) act as a perfect link between the ancient and medieval goldsmith's craft.

5

6

The great state brooch known as the Schaffhausen Onyx (c.1240).

CHAPTER TWO

THE MEDIEVAL CRAFTSMEN

800-1500

The Middle Ages

·

The Byzantine legacy

·

Gothic influences

RONALD LIGHTBOWN

INTRODUCTION

The early Middle Ages – the period from AD 800, when Charlemagne was crowned emperor of the West, to about 1200 – saw the gradual emergence of a distinct European culture out of the confusion of the so-called Dark Ages. With the relative political and economic stability that had been achieved by the 12th century came a wonderful renaissance of artistic and intellectual life, born of the clash of two traditions – the classical tradition and the tradition of native art that had persisted throughout the long centuries of wars and migrations.

The artistic achievements of the Teutonic tribes who

On the reliquary of the head of Saint Elizabeth of Thuringia made of his own drinking-cup, the Emperor Frederick II set his great gold crown, studded with square emeralds and other precious stones. The crown, of closed imperial form, gives some idea of the jewelled magnificence of a 13th century emperor.

swept through Europe remind us that although they might have been barbarians, these people were also capable of producing some of the most beautiful metalwork ever known, whose intricate and mysterious designs appear to us all the more extraordinary because so little is known of the people who created them.

From the age of Charlemagne to around 1200 jewellery designs echoed those of imperial Byzantium. Byzantine art must have been the inspiration of the robes trimmed with broad borders sewn with pearls and stones, the earrings, the bracelets, the heavy collars, the jewelled girdles that we know to have been worn by great men and women in Carolingian and Ottonian times – although not all jewellery worn was as Byzantine as the great gold parure of an imperial lady, dating from about 1000, that was formerly known as the treasure of the Empress Gisela (see page 39). Here the pectoral ornament is wholly Byzantine in style, with its gems strung on long thin wires so that they glittered on the breast like drops of colour. The earrings are of the crescent form popular in the early Middle Ages and are also Byzantine in origin, and the brooch is domed and composed of concentric circles, again probably a Byzantine design. Such great brooches in their stately richness were typical of the majestic jewellery of the early Middle Ages, where the effect sought was one of heavy jewelled splendour produced by the combination of monumentality of form with intricacy of surface decoration, often created by scrolls of filigree sometimes inset with small stones.

The Use of Stones

In the early Middle Ages a greater range of stones was employed in jewellery than was the custom from the beginning of the 13th century. As well as the four great precious stones of the Middle Ages, the sapphire, the ruby, the emerald and the diamond, turquoises and topazes were used, again suggesting Byzantine influence and a taste for a wide variety of colour. We do not know when this taste disappeared, but certainly from about 1200 jewels of gold were principally set with sapphires, rubies, emeralds and diamonds, with pearls in their pure, milky opalescence used for contrast. Of these stones the most highly prized were the sapphire and the ruby, the sapphire being perhaps the more greatly valued up to the 14th century when the ruby rose into high favour. True rubies were comparatively rare; far commoner was the spinel ruby, known in the Middle Ages as the balas ruby after its place of origin, Badakshan in north-eastern Afghanistan.

Although there may have been some limited knowledge of how to cut or shape these stones, before the 14th century they were usually simply polished so that most early medieval stones are cabochon stones, and keep something of the irregularity of their natural form. The art of cutting and faceting stones became much commoner during the 14th century, and during its latter half the art of cutting the diamond was mastered for the first time. At first the cuts were naturally not very elaborate: sapphires and rubies could be cut into eight facets, diamonds into points, and all stones could be table-cut. There is evidence to suggest that much more elaborate cutting and faceting began in the 15th century in the Netherlands, which have since remained the great centre of stone cutting, though the rise of Amsterdam as the capital of the art belongs to a much later period.

Jewels were made in the Middle Ages by goldsmiths rather than by specialist jewellers who only begin to appear in the late 14th century. Stones were set either in collets, or mounted in claw settings *à jour,* a technique that allows light to be reflected through the stone. Stones were tinctured or foiled to improve their colour, and this could and did lead to malpractices that called forth much legislation from the early 13th century onwards. In general, medieval regulations, though seriously concerned with purity and genuineness of metal, reveal less anxiety about the silver and gold used in jewels, since their quantity was small, than about the stones. It was usually forbidden to set gold with semiprecious stones such as amethysts or garnets that were cheaper alternatives for true precious stones, or with the substitute stones of glass and crystal, often tinctured doublets, which were much produced from early times and later became a speciality of Paris. In the cheaper metal silver, on the other hand, it was forbidden to use genuine precious stones. It is plain both from documents and surviving jewels that fraud and deception were extensively practised in the Middle Ages, and that it behoved the purchaser of jewels and precious stones to be on his guard. Sometimes no doubt mistakes were genuine, for gemmology was not yet a very advanced science.

Major Centres and Techniques

The centres for the making of jewellery in the Middle Ages' were the great cities of Paris, Cologne and Venice, with Paris enjoying the supremacy in fashion from about 1200 to 1400 that it was to regain in the 18th and 19th centuries. As goldsmith's work medieval jewellery represents the major goldsmiths' styles of the Middle Ages in miniature: thus 11th- and 12th-century jewellery has the characteristics of Ottonian and Romanesque goldsmiths' work, which in turn reflects the major design styles of its age. The main decorative technique of medieval jewellery was enamelling, in its successive forms: cloisonné enamel derived from Byzantium; *champlevé* enamel; translucent enamel, introduced about 1290; and *émail en ronde bosse,* introduced or revived about 1360. Another source of ornament, used in brooches, was the cameo. Antique cameos were as highly prized and eagerly collected in the Middle Ages as they were in the Renaissance, though not with the same spirit of reverence for the art of antiquity. Brooches like the Schaffhausen Onyx of *c.* 1330–40 show how richly and magnificently such cameos were mounted to make state brooches. Such a brooch would certainly be worn only on great occasions; according to the documents, the best jewellery was for high and holiday wear, and the second-best for more ordinary occasions.

The 13th century, a period of great self-confidence in Western European art, saw notable changes in the style and types of jewellery that were worn. Jewellery seems to have become much lighter in spirit under the influence of the Gothic style, which was first evident in jewellery in the second quarter of the 13th century in Paris, and gradually influenced the style of jewellery elsewhere in Western Europe. For the heavy, rounded forms of earlier jewels it

substituted angular or lobed designs; it replaced their three-dimensional richness with lighter, flatter, two-dimensional designs, in which stones and pearls are isolated against the metal. At the same time earrings and bracelets disappear, except in southern Italy and Sicily, where lingering Byzantine influence, and, in Spain, Moorish influence, kept them in fashion until the end of the Middle Ages. On the heads of noble men and women appears the coronal, or crown, whose distinguishing mark was its fleurons. Lighter and less solemn head ornaments were the chaplet and garland, much worn by wealthy bourgeois men and women as well as by their superiors in degree. Women's hair was bound and wound into tresses and other forms by bands known as *tressoirs* which were often jewelled, sometimes very richly. At the neck was worn a brooch, which might be a simple ring-brooch, at its plainest a plain utilitarian fastener, or a great cluster brooch formed round a cameo. The heavy collars of earlier times disappeared and were replaced by light chains or laces or ribands from which hung pendants, either inside or outside the dress.

Such pendants were often worn to give protection to the wearer. They could take the form of a sacred symbol like a cross, or of a container for holy relics, or of single stones,

This fleur de lis brooch of silver-gilt, probably for a mantle, is decorated with champlevé *enamel and set with stones which are among the earliest cut stones known from the Middle Ages. It dates from the early 14th century. The* fleur-de-lys *was the official badge of the French royal house, and the brooch was preserved among the French royal regalia at the Abbey of Saint-Denis.*

INFLUENCES

This Italian fourteenth century girdle (**1**) of silver parcel gilt and decorated with translucent enamel, shows how the forms of Gothic architecture, as demonstrated in this detail (**2**) of the west façade of Salisbury cathedral, (1220-58), were borrowed by goldsmiths and developed into a miniature ornamental vocabulary for jewellery. When applied to the mounts of a girdle (detail), the style has a fantastic appearance which probably pleased patrons of the 14th century, who sought for gaiety and strangeness in all they wore.

1

2

Set with stones and pearls, these gold earrings of c. 1000 from the Gisela Treasure (3), show the influence of Byzantine jewellery on Imperial German court jewellery. The crescent shape was borrowed from Byzantium, whose imperial dress and jewellery set the fashion for the Emperors of the West.

3

5

4

This circular domed brooch of c.1000 (4), also from the Gisela Treasure, is again probably inspired by Byzantine jewellery. It is of gold, set with stones and pearls, and with a ring of cloisonné enamel round the central sapphire. The effect is monumental, but with a barbaric glow of colour. A 9th

century Byzantine book cover (5) set with pearls, shows the sort of precious Byzantine enamels on gold that were so much admired in the early medieval West. They are executed in the technique of cloisonné, where the enamel colours are separated by fine walls of gold.

EARLY GOLD AND ENAMEL WORK

(**1**) This gold and enamel eagle brooch of c.1000 is part of a treasure of jewels found at Mainz in 1886 which must have belonged to an imperial German lady and was once associated with the Empress Gisela (d.1026) The eagle was a symbol at this period of imperial rule; here it is copied from Byzantium.

1

2

Medieval people frequently wore small pendant crosses of this kind, hung from a lace or chain. This cross (**2**) c.1000, is known as the Dagmar Cross. Made of gold and decorated with cloisonné enamel, it was found in the grave of Queen Dagmar of Denmark (d.1212). It may have come from Byzantium or from South Italy. We are not sure how it reached Denmark, but Byzantine crosses and other ornaments were very popular in Scandinavia.

3

This rich girdle of c.1270 was found on the body of the Infante Fernando de la Cerda (d.1275) son of King Alfonso the Wise of Castile, when his tomb in Las Huelgas, Burgos, was opened (3). The coats-of-arms suggest that it is really English, and was a gift to him, perhaps from Edmund of Lancaster, a son of Henry III. The hoop is for suspending a purse.

4

Ring-brooches were often plain or simply decorated, but they could also be treated as richly showy ornaments. This beautiful, late 13th-century example (4) is of gold, set with sapphires and rubies, with vine leaf scrolls between the collets. It is probably French.

CEREMONIAL JEWELS

1

This reliquary pendant of silver-gilt, set with emeralds, sapphires, rubies and crystals (**1**), was probably made in Bohemia c.1350-70. Under the stones in the lobes are small relics. The engraved flames behind may be the device of St Wenceslas of Bohemia.

(**2**) The Wilton Diptych, painted c.1395, shows Richard II of England wearing a collar of broom-cod, the device of Charles VI of France, and his own device of a white hart, which he assumed in 1390. Badges of this kind were given in the late 14th and 15th century by kings and princes to their intimate household knights and to their relations, friends and supporters. Richard was accused by his opponents of trying to create a faction by his gifts of hart-badges.

2

4

Princess Blanche, daughter of Henry IV, took this English royal crown to Bavaria on her marriage (3). It is of gold, set with rubies, sapphires, diamonds and pearls. The high, spiring pinnacles are typical of late 14th century crowns; this one was made either in France or, more probably, England. Two cloak-clasps (4) of silver gilt and enamel made for King Louis the Great of Hungary and given by him to his chapel in Aachen in about 1374. They show the heraldic magnificence of such ornaments, worn only by the noblest in the land.

3

FIGURATIVE WORK

1

2

The Swan Jewel, from the first half of the 15th century, is of gold, enamelled in the technique of émail en ronde bosse (**1**). It was found in Dunstable. The crown round its neck suggests that it may have been a royal badge, but it may equally have belonged to someone from one of the great English families claiming descent from the Swan Knight. A love of the exotic, one of the leading tastes of fashionable people in the late 14th and early 15th century is exemplified in this dromedary brooch. Of gold, enamelled white and green, it combines intricacy of surface with poetry of feeling and subtlety of workmanship (**2**).

The Langdale rosary (**3**) English, c.1490-1500, is one of only two gold paternosters to survive from the Middle Ages. Its beads are enamelled with the figures of saints, each carefully identified; the larger beads, known as 'gauds', were for marking the number of prayers recited. This magnificent portrait pendant (c.1440) of gold enamelled in the clear red much favoured by later medieval goldsmiths, is set with a hardstone profile of a knight of the Order of the Golden Fleece, probably Duke Philip the Good of Burgundy (**4**). Portrait pendants were rare in the Middle Ages, and were made almost exclusively for French or French-influenced princes and princesses.

3

4

Nicholas Hilliard's exquisite miniature of Anne of Denmark, c. 1603 is contained in an enamelled gold case with gold set diamonds, possibly from the workshop of George Heriot.

CHAPTER · THREE

RENAISSANCE AND BAROQUE JEWELS

1500-1714

Following fine art

·

Classicism

·

The French courts of the Bourbons

·

Death and politics

DIANA SCARISBRICK

INTRODUCTION

The image of the head of St John the Baptist offered on a charger was worn not only as a tribute to his sanctity but was also believed to have curative powers. The Latin inscription round the border of this hat medallion, "Inter natos mulierum non surexsit" ("Among them that are born of women there has not risen a greater"), comes from St Matthew's Gospel, II, v. 11.

Jewellery in the Renaissance reached an artistic level comparable to that achieved in the fine arts. Artists as distinguished as Albrecht Dürer, Hans Holbein and Giulio Romano were commissioned by princely patrons to produce designs which stimulated goldsmiths to bring their traditional skills of enamelling, chasing and casting to heights never since equalled. New motifs derived from classical art joined the medieval themes of religion and sentiment, which were re-interpreted.

The lead came from Italy, where the elegant but conservative designs of the 15th century were transformed into the exuberant and sculptural style associated with Benvenuto Cellini (1502–/2). In his *Autobiography* Cellini recalls the fashion for hat badges in Rome at the outset of his career, successors to the medieval pilgrim and livery badges and, like them, worn in the upturned brim of the hat. Chased or embossed with scenes from the Bible, or from classical mythology or history, they declared cultural interests or spiritual aspirations. Modelled in gold, bright with enamels and highlighted with coloured gemstones and diamonds, they represent the fully evolved Renaissance style of jewellery. By the end of the 16th century

this sculptural, historiated style had given way to flatter, more decorative jewels in which stones play the principal role. An example of the latter is a heart-shaped hat jewel enclosing the ruby initials "DM" amidst blue forget-me-nots which was found in the tomb of Count Otto Heinrich of Neuberg (1556–1604) at Lauingen on the Danube. His wife, Dorothea Maria, put it there.

Although the openwork style of the heart was new, the ornamental use of personal ciphers was not. Holbein's jewellery designs of the 1530s include a pendant with the initials "HI" for Henry VIII and Queen Jane Seymour, and "RE", perhaps for Enricus Rex. Mary Tudor owned a diamond necklace composed of "P"'s and "M"'s for herself and her husband, Philip II of Spain, and James I wore a hat badge with his wife's initial, "A" for Anne, likewise studded with diamonds. Holbein's historiated jewels carry longer inscriptions, and both necklaces and bracelets might be composed of letters spelling out messages in Latin or the vernacular, wrought in gold or studded with stones. The most prestigious of these monogram jewels were religious in character, representing the abbreviated Greek name of Christ, IHS, in Gothic or Roman capitals, and set with diamonds, the back enamelled with the Instruments of Christ's Passion – crown of thorns, nails, scourge and ladder. These were worn by Protestant men and women, who also wore crosses. Devotional jewellery reflecting Roman Catholic practices, especially veneration of the Virgin Mary, was restricted to those remaining loyal to the Papacy, particularly in Spain, where jewelled badges of the religious Confraternities were a speciality.

Secular pendants pinned to the sleeve or hung from the neck demonstrate the diversity of Renaissance culture. They illustrate episodes from classical literature such as the stories of Diana and Actaeon, of Leda and the Swan, of Apollo and Daphne, of Cupid, busy firing his arrows at human hearts. Allegorical figures were popular: Charity with her children, Faith with her cross, Fortitude with her column, and in the last quarter of the 16th century they were contained in architectural settings in a style associated with the German designer Hans Collaert. The asymmetrical and distorted shapes of baroque pearls presented a particular challenge to the imagination as well as the technical skills of the Renaissance goldsmith, who transformed them into magnificent mermaids and tritons, warriors in armour, lions, rabbits and wounded stags.

The Classical Influences

The classical revival, which provided the goldsmith with a vocabulary of divinities, nymphs, satyrs, heroes, pediments and volutes, also brought with it a return to the difficult courtly art of gem engraving. Both intaglios – for signet rings – and cameos were set in Renaissance hat jewels, pendants, bracelets and necklaces, in wrought-gold and jewelled frames. Some are reinterpretations of Roman themes – emperors and empresses, patriots and heroes – but others show an independent attitude to classical prototypes and are illustrations of events from the Bible or portraits of illustrious Renaissance men and women in contemporary dress. Rulers awarded their cameo portraits as a mark of the highest distinction: less rare, but almost as highly regarded, were miniatures in jewelled cases and medallic portraits, known as badges of honour, worn on long gold chains.

It was said that Sir Thomas Gresham, the founder of the Royal Exchange, invested his entire fortune in gold chains, and certainly every man and woman of standing wore them, in single or multiple rows and made of a variety of links, including knots imitating those in the ropes tied round the habits of Franciscan friars. Also worn at the neck were carcanets composed of richly chased and enamelled gold links set with gemstones in high bezels, usually alternating with groups of milky-white pearls. Although narrower versions of these might be worn on the wrists, most bracelets were in the form of gold chains, individualized with ciphers, coats of arms and the betrothal symbols of hearts and hands on the clasps.

In the northern countries women's hair was covered with a French hood embellished with two rows of jewellery, known as biliments, and since the ears were covered, earrings were rare. But well before 1600 the French hood was out of fashion, and bodkins and aigrettes – like tufts of feathers – were pinned in hair padded out artificially and crowned with an "attire" of pearls strung into lace-like patterns on a wire frame. Besides earrings of pear pearls, there were others of goldsmith's work: ciphers, blackamoors, dolphins and mermaids playing the lute.

Women's dresses, enriched by sets of buttons, were belted with jewelled bands matching carcanets, bracelets and biliments, or with rows of agate nuts sometimes enclosing figurative scenes. Hanging from the neck and girdle were useful items which the Renaissance goldsmith made into jewels: whistles designed as dragons, toothpicks like eagles' claws, fans with jewelled handles, fur-pieces with wrought-gold sable heads, and pomanders to scent the foul air.

Portraits show rings worn in profusion, and at no period have designs ever been so diverse. There are gimmel rings with double-hoop and twin bezels, symbolic of the married state, locket rings enclosing minute portraits, superb diamond rings made for royalty, signets engraved with complicated coats of arms, and each exemplifies the artistic spirit of the Renaissance.

The Rise of the Gemstone

In the 17th century this close connection with the fine arts came to an end as the craft of the jeweller was increasingly concerned with the display of stones rather than with the expression of intellectual con-

cepts, rank, occupation, religion or political allegiance. From the reign of Henri IV and Marie de Medici Paris was acknowledged as the centre of taste and fashion. This ascendancy was confirmed by the splendour of Versailles under their grandson, Louis XIV. French designs were diffused abroad through pattern books, and the Revocation of the Edict of Nantes in 1685 drove so many Huguenot craftsmen out of France that in 1706 the Dowager Duchesse d'Orléans could observe that it was no longer true that pretty things had to be bought in Paris.

The supply of gemstones increased during the 17th century but especially after the 1660s, when the East India Company gave the Marranos Portuguese Jews established in London permission to trade independently. At the same time the discovery of the laws of refraction and of the principles of analytical geometry stimulated progress in faceting and polishing. The rose cut with multiple facets had

This decorative hat jewel was recorded by Hans Mielich in the pictorial inventory of the collection of Duke Albrecht V of Bavaria and his wife, Duchess Anna. The gemstones and pearls are mounted in a design of oak branches with acorns enlivened by small figures – pairs of birds, lizards and dragons – darting between the settings. The raised six-sided collets are engraved and enamelled, an innovation of the 1540s.

INTRODUCTION

Figurative pendants express cultural and spiritual interests. A Pelican in her Piety, piercing her breast to feed her young, symbolizes Christ's sacrifice on the cross, it is also an allegory for Charity. The boyish figure of Cupid shooting his arrows comes from classical mythology, and the toothpick representing the heroine Lucretia recalls the event, recorded in Livy's history of Rome, which led to the establishment of the Republic in 509 BC. The onyx cameo of two men, probably brothers, represents the revival of the ancient art of gem engraving.

succeeded the elementary point – and table – cut early in the 17th century, and then in the 1660s the brilliant cut became available, releasing more light from the diamond than ever before. To avoid yellow reflections silver settings were substituted for gold which was then used for coloured stones only. Often combined with diamonds, these coloured stones were both precious – emeralds, sapphires and rubies – and semiprecious – amethysts, chrysoberyls, peridots, turquoises, topazes, coral, jet and opals. Pearls, if white, round and flawless, were more prized than any of these, and were threaded in the hair, hung from the ears, worn next to the skin round the neck and wrists, and set in jewels.

Substitutes for pearls and coloured stones could be obtained in Paris and Venice, while colourless crystals which could be faceted were a cheap alternative to diamonds. Not only were figurative elements banished from settings but the role of enamel was much reduced except in watch cases and lockets. Thanks to a technique invented by the Toutin family of Blois, flat surfaces could be enamelled with still-life, topographical and genre scenes and reproductions of the Baroque canvases of Simon Vouet and Charles Lebrun – continuing the 16th-century association between the fine arts and personal ornaments.

Pattern books reflect the contemporary passion for botany and plant life. Balthasar Lemersier's *Bouquets d'Orfevrerie* (1626) contains variations on the theme of pea-pod plants – called *cosse de pois* – with sprays of leaves shooting upwards and curved round petal-shaped settings for gemstones. A more naturalistic style was developed by Johann Paul Hauer in 1650, and then, in tune with the classicism of Versailles, acanthus leaves became a dominant theme.

The Hair Jewels of the Mid-17th Century

I n the middle of the 17th century only a few jewels were worn with the hair fashions of the day: the face was framed with ringlets and a string of pearls might be entwined in the chignon and bodkins placed at the sides. These were ornamented with jewelled insects like butterflies, dragonflies, snails and caterpillars perched on long stems, or with shepherds' crooks and flowers studded with rose-cut diamonds and cabochon gemstones. In contrast, by the 1690s, large floral sprays with stems bent under the weight of diamonds and pearls emphasized the tall, padded coiffures that were worn with feathers dyed to match the ribbons tied in bows on the dress. The high pleated, stiffened lace "Fontanges" head-dresses, which originated at Versailles, also sparkled with clusters of faceted stones scattered on the front and sides of the head. Men's hats were encircled by bands of gemstones or gold chains and strings of pearls. The aigrette remained in fashion until it was superseded by the button and loop holding up the brim around 1700.

Notwithstanding the immense popularity of pear pearls at this time, some earrings were made of gemstones and goldsmith's work. Amethysts carved into bunches of grapes which probably date from the middle of the century were found in the Cheapside Hoard (the stock of a jeweller discovered on a site in Cheapside in London in 1912), and there must have been other such imaginative designs. Most characteristic of the period is the girandole, consisting of a top cluster with three pendants branching out like the arms of a candelabra and sometimes linked to the main-cluster by a ribbon bowknot.

Large natural pearls, evenly matched like peas in a pod, were most sought after for necklaces, which were tied at the back with ribbon bows. But the diamond, with its new brilliance, had asserted its pre-eminence by the time of the coronation of Queen Anne in London in 1702, when many peeresses wore necklaces of rose-cut stones simply set in heavy silver mounts with one or two rows falling in front like festoons. A role was found for enamel on chains and necklaces: some were composed of plaques painted with landscapes and allegorical figures, of blue, black and white bowknots, and red stars, each centred on a pearl.

Men prided themselves on their insignia, jewelled buttons, and miniatures or badges of honour hanging from gold chains. An innovation with a long future ahead of it was the sleeve button, designed to fasten the cuff at each

The back of this diamond-studded miniature case, c.1610–20, is enamelled with a crowned red heart transfixed by arrows and inscribed in French "Fidel iusq a la mort le pareil de vous a mon confort" ("Faithful unto death your likeness is my comfort").

wrist and replacing the ribbon used until then. These appear in England in the late 1660s.

In the first half of the 17th century women of fashion almost invariably wore a large jewel in the centre of the corsage. Hélène Fourment wears a large gold and diamond jewel of *cosse de pois* design with long jewelled stems shooting upwards around a central cluster, in a portrait *c.* 1630 painted by her husband, Rubens. These, like crosses, might be pinned over a ribbon bowknot, but from the middle of the 17th century the bowknot was interpreted in metal and gemstones, ultimately being combined with acanthus scrolls, following Versailles fashion. Brandenburgs, of oblong form, inspired by the frogging on the jackets of Prussian soldiers and worn as one large jewel or in graduated sets down to the waist, were another Versailles fashion which was taken up internationally. In the interests of a uniformly elegant toilette, brooches, buttons, sleeve clasps, earrings, necklaces and aigrettes were increasingly being made in sets of matching design and material, evolving into the 18th-century parure.

Two constant themes in 17th-century jewellery were death and politics. The successive constitutional crises in England are evoked by rings, brooches, lockets and bracelet slides – worn on velvet bands passing through loops at the back – representing Charles I and his children, and then William and Mary. Memorial jewels commemorating private individuals are of similar design: they are ornamented with *memento mori* symbols – skulls and cross-bones, hour-glasses and coffins – and often contain locks of hair identified with ciphers worked in gold wire.

INFLUENCES

The architecture of the Italian Renaissance was gradually adopted in northern countries beyond the Alps; in France, for example, François I and Henri II built the palace of Fontainebleau around a series of courts in the classical style, here illustrated in a drawing by Jacques Ducerceau, c. 1570 (*2*). In jewellery, one of the ways in which classicism was expressed was in the revival of the ancient art of engraving hardstones in relief. This sardonyx cameo (*1*) of Omphale wearing the lion-skin of her lover, Hercules, set in a gold jewelled pendant, was given by the Hapsburg emperor Charles V to the Medici pope Clement VII.

1

2

3

4

5

The Protestant Reformation did not bring the medieval custom of wearing devotional jewellery to an end. The most powerful of Christian symbols – the cross – was brought up to date: here table-cut diamonds are set in raised quatrefoil collets, whose sides are chased with crescents outlined in enamel (3). Episodes from the Old and New Testaments were wrought in enamelled gold highlighted with gemstones. Don John of Austria is said to have worn this hat badge (4) depicting the Conversion of St Paul and these miniature jewelled tableaux (5) are the goldsmith's versions of religious paintings such as Jacopo Bassano's Way of Calvary, c. 1540.

PENDANTS AND ACCESSORIES

*Illustrating the international court style is a Portuguese crown jewel, a pendent scent bottle in the form of a lion with ruby eyes, jewelled collar and naturalistically chased mane and coat studded with table- and rose-cut diamonds (**1**). The diamond heart held in the forepaws is inscribed in Italian "Qui soggiorna che gire ancor". The head unscrews so the scent can perfume foul air. Scent bottles and pomanders hung from the girdle or on chains round the neck.*

1

3

2

*The lion with milky-white baroque pearl set in his body contrasts with the gleaming gilt head, forepaws and hindquarters (**2**). Every gemstone in the Renaissance had a magical property assigned to it. To make sure that the "virtues" of the peridot and hessonite garnet framed in acanthus (**3**) are transmitted directly to the skin, the back of the pendant has been left open.*

Toothpicks were just as essential to personal comfort as scent and were likewise made into jewels. This mermaid's torso is set with a baroque pearl whose swelling curves simulate feminine contours, and her fish tail is enamelled with a green scale-pattern and terminates in the pick (**4**). The sculptural skills of the goldsmith developed so that now several figures could be grouped together in one jewel, often contained in an architectural setting. The Adoration of the Magi is here enacted on a stage framed with ruby obelisks on diamond bases beneath an arch. The diamond star of Bethlehem shines above the Virgin and Child, who are raised on a throne (**5**).

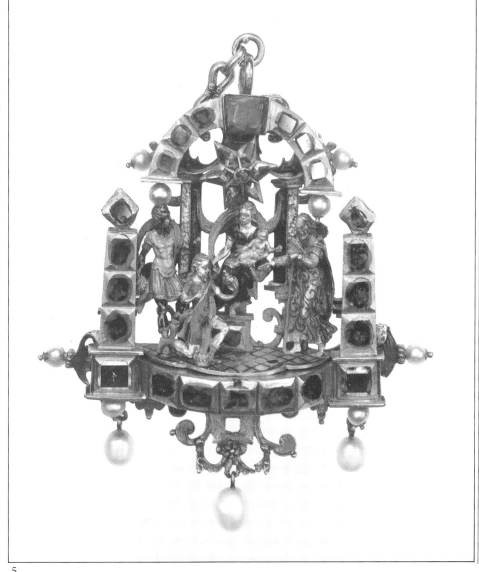

4   5

COLLARS

HANS HOLBEIN

Monogram and lyre pendants of classical character designed by Hans Holbein.

Hans Holbein, in England from 1532 to 1543, designed hat badges, pendants, rings, girdle books and chains which incorporate classical motifs: masks, cornucopiae, acanthus leaves and arabesques. Some of them are figurative, illustrating events from mythology or the Bible, such as the wife of Lot turning into a pillar of salt. Inscriptions give an individual charm to Holbein's designs: a lyre-shaped pendant enclosing flowers is inscribed in Latin "Quam accipere dare multo beatus" ("How much better it is to give than to receive"). Holbein classicized the medieval cipher jewel by entwining it with acanthus leaves: the pendant in the form of RE, set with coloured stones and hung with pearls, may refer to Henry VIII – Enricus Rex. Most of these designs are now in the British Museum and, along with contemporary portraits, are all that we have to tell us of early Tudor court jewellery.

Hans Mielich, court painter to Duke Albrecht V of Bavaria, recorded the jewels of the duke and duchess in a pictorial inventory. One of the grandest of all the magnificent pieces illustrated was this collar (2) of wrought gold, enamelled in bright colours and set with gemstones alternating with pairs of pearls in floral frames, and with figures of satyrs and nymphs seated in cartouches. Each link is a jewel in its own right. A cross of similar style hangs from the collar with the date 1554. Fifty years later the figurative elements have gone, the enamelling is much more sober and diamonds and pearls play the dominant role in this caracanet and the openwork pendant hanging from it (1) from the imperial castle of Ambras. Made by a Hapsburg court jeweller they illustrate the transition from the figurative style of the Renaissance to the 17th-century emphasis on gemstones.

SENTIMENT IN JEWELLERY

In 17th-century jewellery the heart is used as a religious emblem as well as a sign of personal sentiment. The enamelled gold locket (**1**) set with table-cut rubies and diamonds is centred on a ruby heart transfixed by Cupid's arrows and crowned with diamonds – the reward of fidelity. The back (**2**), which is enamelled with flowers and leaves, contains the miniature of a man.

1 2

Representative of the Prague court style, this is said to have belonged to Rakóczy, Prince of Transylvania. An arrow, alluding to Cupid, whose attribute it is, is set with emeralds and rose-cut diamonds; the point with table-cut garnets might be worn in the hair (**3**).

3

4

Cupid is depicted taking aim with a diamond-tipped arrow and ruby bow in a pendant (4) similar to one listed among the jewels of Queen Anna Christina of Denmark in 1597: his body is studded with gemstones and there is a pearl in his ear.

The heart motif was also adopted for rings and held by a hand is applied here (5) to the shoulders of a gimmel ring. Gimmel means twin, from the Latin gemellus, and the ring has twin hoops terminating in a double bezel, an allegory of the married state. The hoops are inscribed in Latin with the words from St Matthew's Gospel that affirm the indissolubility of Christian marriage: "Let not man put asunder what God has joined together". The infant and the skeleton in cavities within the bezel refer to man's pilgrimage through life which he begins as a naked baby and ends when, naked once more, he returns to God (6).

5

6

BOTANICAL THEMES

Many 17th-century jewels are enamelled with patterns of flowers like miniature Dutch still-life paintings. A magnificent watch case (**1**) – probably made for a member of a royal family – with tulips, daisies and lilies worked in relief in opaque white highlighted with black on a bluish-green ground encloses a movement by the Parisian watchmaker Jehan Cremsdorff. The top cover is set with table-cut diamonds round the circumference converging in six lines on a centre stone. Allegorical figures of Charity and Hope ornament the insides of the covers, and there is another on the dial.

1

Large numbers of small diamonds are set in a gold cosse de pois (pea-pod) style breast ornament (**3**) composed of long-stemmed plants curved round a central cluster, and hung with five pendants. This jewel is close to the designs of Balthasar Lemersier, and in a portrait of c. 1630 Rubens' wife is wearing a similar jewel. Long enamelled chains (**4**) composed of flowers or leaves were among the stock of a mid 17th-century jeweller that was discovered by chance on a site in Cheapside in London in 1912. Of the 35 chains in the hoard the majority were of floral design.

3

2

The English court style is illustrated by the enamelled gold case (**2**) containing a miniature of Sir Bevil Grenville who died fighting for Charles I in 1643. The floral pattern stands out brilliantly against the black ground embellished with precious stones.

4

DECORATIVE MOTIFS

Inspired by the coloured ribbons which trimmed dresses during the 17th century jewellers created bowknot jewels, most of them for the breast, but also as necklaces with links enamelled in opaque colours and centred on a large bowknot studded with diamonds and hung with a sapphire drop (1).

MEMENTO MORI

The 17th century was a time of political unrest, long wars and periodic outbreaks of plague. Religious attitudes and much of literature emphasized the brevity of this life compared with eternity. This was expressed in jewels ornamented with motifs which represented familiar concepts of the passing of time, such as the winged hour-glass, coffins, infants blowing bubbles, skulls and cross-bones. In the second half of the century *memento mori* symbols were combined with jewels worn in memory of specific individuals. In England a large category

of *memento mori* jewels commemorated King Charles I, executed in 1649, and venerated as a martyr by royalists

Ring, with skull and cross-bones framed in rubies, may have originally been set with diamonds in the eye sockets and nostrils.

4

2

3

In the designs of the itinerant English jeweller Marcus Gunter acanthus, laden with rose-cut stones and hung with briolettes, is the dominant motif. His aigrette (2) with a long pin to fix in the hair was designed in Amsterdam in 1711; the girandole earrings (3) with triple pendants hanging from the top setting were made in Siena and are dated 1703.

Cross-bones ornament the suspension chains of a coffin pendant (4) enamelled and hung with skulls and more cross-bones. Inside the coffin a white skeleton is accompanied by the dramatic inscription in German which translated means "Here I lie and wait for you I.G.S."

Radiated brooch in stylized flower shape, diamonds set in silver, dated c. 1770.

CHAPTER · FOUR

ELEGANCE AND ROMANTICISM

1715-1836

The Georgians

·

The Rococo movement

·

The Napoleonic Empire

·

Neoclassicism and revivals

DIANA SCARISBRICK

INTRODUCTION

The badge of the Knights of St John of Jerusalem, rulers of the island of Malta from 1530. The Maltese cross was adopted by jewellers in London after the confirmation of British sovereignty by the Treaty of Paris in 1814. Set with diamonds, this cross would have hung from a necklace similarly set, or from a velvet ribbon.

A distinction was made at the beginning of the 18th century between the jewels worn with informal daytime clothes and the grander ornaments – or parures – required with full dress. Since better lighting made it possible for important social occasions to take place at night, "dress" jewels were designed to look their best by candlelight.

The emphasis on stones rather than settings continued to increase, and improved faceting showed off the full beauty of diamonds and coloured stones in lighter, more informal and delicate designs in tune with the elegant rococo spirit. The traditional source of gemstones in India was supplemented by imports of diamonds from Brazil, eclipsing pearls, though these were still much worn. Not only sparkle was expected of jewels, but also deep flashes of colour, achieved by expert foiling, while some jewellers, notably G.F. Strass of Paris, successfully tinted diamonds. France remained the fount of inspiration for style and craftsmanship, which were upheld abroad by the Huguenots and by Parisian jewellers invited to work at foreign courts: J.F. Fistaine in Copenhagen, Louis Duval in St Petersburg, and Augustin Duflos in Madrid. Engravings by designers such as Mondon and Pouget diffused French fashions further, and since clients everywhere acknowledged their superiority, fine jewellery was international in character.

Seventeenth–century designs were brought up to date: aigrettes and ornamental insects – moths, flies and butterflies – for the hair, girandole earrings, bowknots for the bodice. Acanthus was discarded, asymmetry was introduced and ribbonwork became more fluid and intricate, interspersed with flowers. This naturalistic trend continued into the late Georgian period, then after 1761 Neo-classical fret (or key pattern), honeysuckle and husks appear, contained in compact geometrical forms which, although more severe, still have the elegance of the rococo. Enamel disappears from the backs of settings which from the 1760s are backed with gold, thus avoiding tarnish.

It is in daytime jewellery that enamel finds a continuing role, decorating chatelaines, watch and miniature cases, lockets and bracelet clasps. From the 1760s a distinctive blue was used to outline settings and cover the plaques for ciphers on bracelets and rings, the rich colour contrasting well with the bright gold lustre. Memorial and sentimental jewellery was another daytime favourite. Hair, plaited or worked into mesh-like patterns, was incorporated into brooches, rings, bracelet clasps and pendants hung from chains at the neck, identified with ciphers and framed in small pearls or enamelled borders sometimes inscribed with loving messages such as "inseparable jusqu'à la mort". From the 1770s the fichu at the neck might be fastened with an oval-shaped brooch with a love motif: flaming torches, twinned hearts, padlocks and Cupid himself.

Naturalistic sprigs of flowers were placed in the hair and also birds, paved with diamonds and pecking at berries or holding out emerald olive branches. Much to Neo-classical taste in the latter half of the 18th century were jewelled stars, crescents, feathers and, later, tiaras, which were worn over the brow in the manner of a Roman empress. The large hats then fashionable were pinned with brooches, some themselves designed as miniature hats ornamented with trophies of love and of the arts.

Whether she was in "dress" or "undress", earrings were essential to the appearance of the well-dressed woman. Suitable for day wear were clusters made from cheap materials, especially *coq de perle* from periwinkle shells, and paste in colours matching the dress or trimmings, sold *en suite* with a demi-parure brooch or cross. For evening the elaborate girandole with its triple pendants now linked to the top by ribbonwork with flowers remained a favourite, and single–drop earrings grew to five centimetres (two inches) in length, balancing hair worn high and topped with nodding plumes.

Diamonds were reserved for evening necklaces, and the *rivière* of graduated stones was the most prestigious of all designs. Smaller stones were worked into intricate garlands of flowers and ribbons with an esclavage or long loop hanging down from the section encircling the neck. Simpler styles were composed of clusters in rows or jewelled bowknots sewn on a velvet choker worn high on the throat. From the 1770s new motifs were derived from curtain and upholstery trimmings: lines of stones hanging in festoons or set in pendent tassels.

Courtly Jewels

Eighteenth-century court dress was embellished with magnificent stomachers filling the space between the neckline and the waist. The scale presented a challenge to jewellers, who created the large bouquets and bowknots simulating floral-patterned ribbons which are

the great triumphs of rococo craftsmanship. Smaller brooches made *en suite* were pinned to the sleeves or scattered over the skirt, their glittering effect enhanced by the rich fabric underneath.

The same high standard of fashionable design and quality was applied to jewels of less expensive materials: bright red cornelian, moss-agate and garnets, which were foiled to glow like warm rose-red rubies. Substitutes widely used included pinchbeck, a gilt metal invented by a Fleet Street watchmaker, and paste. White and coloured paste

was almost universally used for buttons, and for buckles on shoes, garters and belts. In Switzerland, where diamonds were forbidden by the sumptuary laws, marcasite was cut into small stones, faceted and polished to shine attractively by candlelight. From the 1760s marcasite was combined with cut steel, a speciality of Matthew Boulton of Birmingham, who exported it all over Europe in chatelaines, pendants, bracelets, brooches, belt clasps, earrings, dress combs and buttons. Cut steel also combined well with Staffordshire enamels and with the ceramic plaques made by Josiah Wedgwood representing characters and events from antiquity as well as from contemporary literature and history, the white figures standing out in relief against the tinted ground like cameos. Another cheap, mass-produced material used extensively for rings and bracelets was the coloured-glass paste made by the Scot James Tassie reproducing ancient and modern engraved gems.

The 18th-century man of fashion also delighted in jewellery. While the privileged few had their magnificent insignia of the Orders of Chivalry for court dress, all gentlemen might expect to carry a sword with jewelled hilt and wear good rings, a fine watch with wrought-gold seal, and a locket or miniature hanging from a chain round the neck. A jewelled pin held the cravat in place, sleeve links fastened the cuffs, and there were paste or cut-steel buckles on shoes, garters and belt. Buttons – in sets – were essential for the well-trimmed suit, and these – enamelled or set with gems or paste – might also indicate cultural and sporting interests. As dress became plainer after the 1770s so did buttons become excessively large.

The Emergence of Neo-classicism

A simplification of dress, with correspondingly less emphasis on jewellery, marked the years of political change which followed the French Revolution of 1789 whose effects were felt throughout Europe. However, the emergence of Napoleon as Emperor of France in 1804 brought about a revival in the art of jewellery as he determined to outshine his Bourbon predecessors by pomp and display. The rich Neo-classical Empire style devised for this purpose by the painter David was applied to the creation of fabulous parures worn by the women of the imperial family on numerous state occasions. Their tiaras, earrings, necklaces, bracelets and brooches of Greek fret, honeysuckle, palmettes and wreaths of vine and laurel, studded with diamonds, emeralds, rubies and engraved gems from the former royal collection, set the standard for the rest of Europe. Although the classical motifs were rejected by the Bourbons after their return to power in 1815 the rich style was not, and the Napoleonic parures were transformed into the equally grandiose scrolled and botanical designs of the Restoration. These were also emulated abroad, particularly in England, where the

J. J. Rousseau's novel, La Nouvelle Héloïse *(1761), exalting sentiment and virtue in contrast to the artificiality of fashionable life, promoted the wearing of sentimental jewellery, particularly by day. This shuttle-shaped ring contains a lock of hair identified by a cipher.*

INFLUENCES

Madame de Pompadour was known for her exquisite taste and, as mistress of Louis XV, could command the greatest artistic talents of France. In a portrait (3) by François Boucher, her favourite painter, she epitomizes 18th-century elegance. She was also the patroness of the gem engraver Jacques Guay and commissioned cameos and intaglios from him for bracelet clasps. The subjects usually refer to contemporary French history.

1

2

3

This cornelian intaglio (2) of Louis XV as Hercules between Victory and Peace, is inscribed "Preliminaires de la paix 1748". Framed in diamond olive branches it fastened Madame de Pompadour's pearl bracelet. She learnt to cut cameos herself, and the portrait of Louis XV is her own work which she wore in a ring (1).

72

4

Nostalgia for the Middle Ages and the Renaissance was an aspect of Romanticism which found expression in costume balls where guests impersonated historical characters. One of the most famous of such events was the Quadrille Mary Stuart held at the Tuileries by the Duchesse de Berri in 1829, when a visit of Mary of Guise from Scotland to the court of François II and her daughter Mary Stuart in 1559 was re-enacted. An album of water-colours by Eugène Lami recorded the costumes (6), and the duchess was given a necklace and pair of bracelets enamelled with miniatures of some of the most successful (4). In London the Marchioness of Londonderry opened Holdernesse House with a costume ball, where, dressed as Queen Elizabeth and covered with jewels, she greeted her guests seated on a throne (5).

The Marchioness of Londonderry

In the Costume of QUEEN ELIZABETH as worn at the Ball at the Opening of Holderness House

Published by Whitaker & Co in La Belle Assemblée Nº 66 (new series) for June 1830
and by M Colnaghi Nº 23, Cockspur St. Charing Cross

5

6

RINGS

1

Rings provided the final touch of elegance to the toilette. This group includes openwork sprays of flowers, tied with ribbons or placed in a vase, set with small rose-cut diamonds or coloured stones, known as "giardinetti". Love rings are designed round the heart motif: single, twinned, bound together by a golden band, and crowned with diamonds. The enamelled carnival mask centre recalls one of the favourite amusements of 18th-century society, the masquerade or masked ball (1). In contrast to these light-hearted trifles Neo-classical rings are more solid and serious. Here, the golden figure of Diana on a lapis-blue ground derives from a famous intaglio at Naples signed by the Roman court engraver Dioscourides, and the polished sardonyx is a perfect specimen, resembling an eye (2).

2

3

5

7

4

6

8

Another hardstone much admired was moss-agate, with inclusions simulating the branches of trees or even landscapes, which was set in rings and framed in diamonds (5). Love rings were set not only with ruby hearts (1) but also with emeralds contrasting with diamonds, and bound together and crowned (3). The wedding ring was usually a gold band with a love poem or posy inside, which might be protected by a keeper, such as the diamond hoop worn by Queen Charlotte, wife of George III, of which this (7) is a copy. Diamonds might be set in rows (7) or in cluster bezels (6) supported by gold hoops which divided at the shoulders and sometimes enclosed a leaf or flower. Miniatures were now small enough to wear in rings: that of Augustus the Strong, King of Poland and Elector of Saxony, is richly framed in diamonds (8). Neo-Classical sentiment which developed under the influence of Jean Jacques Rousseau was expressed in large rings containing the hair of a loved one, living or dead, framed in deep blue and white borders and rimmed with pearls (4).

ROCOCO FLOWERS

Flowers are the principal theme in rococo jewellery as they are in the other decorative arts of the period. French designers, such as J.H. Pouget in Traité des Pierres Precieuses (1762), published many designs for floral jewels. A choker (**1**) consists of a garland of coloured pastes—even the richest women did not spurn paste.

1

2

3

Expert foiling produced colours such as the deep red and green in the single flower brooch (**2**). Some delightful creations are hat brooches pinned with sprays of flowers combined with feathers and trophies of love and music (**3**).

4

Sometimes enamel was combined with gemstones as in a large, realistically modelled bouquet (6) donated to the Sanctuary of the Virgin of the Pillar at Saragossa (by Dona Juana Rabasa). The deep blue

bouquets and festoons enamelled on the book plate and suspension chains of an English chatelaine of c. 1760 make a striking contrast with the bright gold ground (4).

Sprays of flowers and leaves might soften the favourite double cluster style of earring (5) which lit up the face from the sides.

5

6

RUBIES AND GARNETS

Colour, which was such an important element in 18th-century jewellery, was provided by precious stones, enamel and paste. The warm red of rubies is enhanced by the white light of diamonds in a pair of bracelets (**1**) composed of two rows of clusters between lines of diamonds.

An equally effective contrast is provided less expensively by garnets and lemon-yellow chrysolites or topazes which enliven an aigrette (**3**) worn to the side of tall padded hair and pinned to nodding ostrich plumes.

Equally successful is the combination of rubies, topazes, emeralds and diamonds in a pair of girandole earrings (**2**), the triple drops linked by leafy sprays of flowers. Under the patronage of the empresses of Russia the jewellers of St Petersburg created such rich interpretations of the rococo style as the ruby and diamond spray (**4**) made in c. 1750–1770 which is a tour de force of setting, for the stones have been massed together in a mosaic of colour and light with almost no metal showing.

1

2

3

4

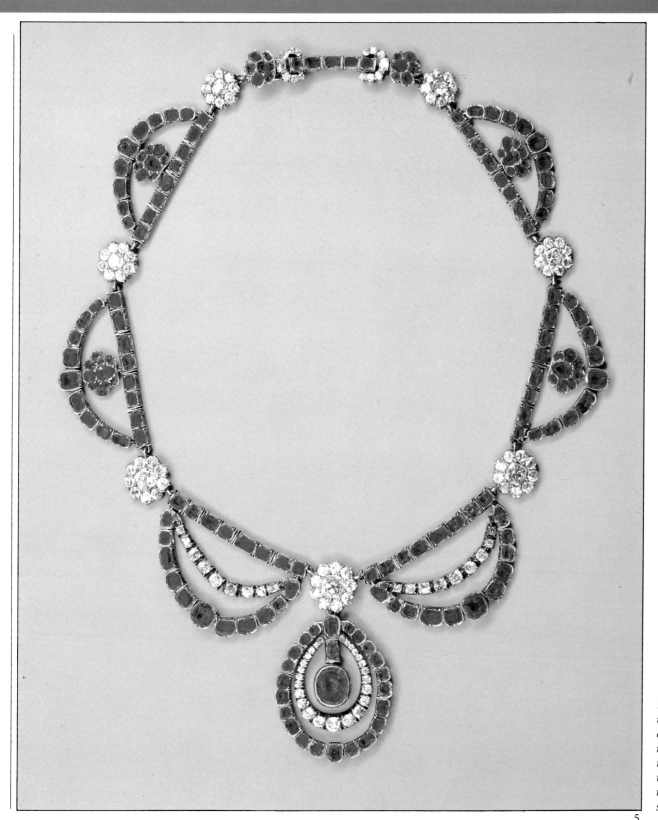

Low necklines were de rigueur *with court dress and left space for elegant compositions such as this ruby and diamond necklace (5) intersected by clusters and hung with festoons culminating in a ruby pendant. The diamonds are set in silver, the rubies in gold.*

5

ROMANTICISM

Glass mosaic and gold parure of necklace, comb and earrings (belt clasp missing) c. 1810. The medallions represent Pompeian bird and butterfly motifs and a spaniel in a landscape, and were a Roman speciality, being made by craftsmen trained in the Vatican workshops making murals and floors in the ancient tradition. Like cameos engraved in hardstone or shell glass mosaic jewellery was acquired by visitors as a souvenir of travel (**1**).

1

Regional Specialities

Coral carved into beads or cameos could be bought in Naples and Genoa, and in Florence ornaments inlaid with hardstones in decorative patterns. North of the Alps the Swiss excelled at enamelling. Watchcases, chains sold well, but it was the bracelets composed of plaques showing young women dressed in the costumes of the respective cantons which most appealed to British travellers, who compared

Berlin Iron Gothic Revival bracelet c. 1830.

them with the drab agricultural and urban worker's dress at home. Ivory carving of sporting subjects came from the Black Forest: these were made up into earrings, bracelets and brooches. From Berlin came severe black ornaments cast in the foundries in classical designs with honeysuckle, fret and moulded replicas of cameos. After 1820 Gothic ornament: ogival arches, rose windows and trefoils predominate.

2

3

The snake, emblem of eternity and symbol of wisdom was worn by both men and women in jewels during the Romantic period and after. The coils looked well round the arm in bracelets, enamelled blue, with diamond heads and ruby eyes (2). Eighteenth-century

naturalism never went out of fashion, but was transformed into richer more colourful compositions such as this demi-parure (3) of brooch and earrings, the gemstones being set in bright yellow gold "antique style".

ROMANTICISM

Crowned emperor in 1806, Napoleon sought to impose his authority by a great show of pomp and luxury. Such was his success that after the Restoration of 1815 the Bourbon monarchy – who also wished to impress and command respect – adopted the same grandiose style of jewellery with large stones set in substantial mounts, unambiguously declaring wealth and status. This is the background to the necklace of a graduated double row of sapphires set round with diamonds, worn with earrings en suite (*1*). For daytime wear long chains were hung across the shoulders and hooked at the waist with a watch or lorgnette. They were usually made of pinchbeck with links of different designs stamped with stars. This chain (*2*) is fastened by a pair of hands, beringed and emerging from rose-patterned cuffs.

1

Mid-19th century locket-back, gold pendant with a garnet cabochon,
surrounded by a diamond-set, white and green enamelled cartouche frame

CHAPTER FIVE

VICTORIANA AND BELLE EPOQUE

1837-1914

The art jeweller

·

The Industrial Revolution

·

Diamond refinement

·

Mourning pieces

PETER HINKS

INTRODUCTION

A gold, Roman mosaic and onyx cameo locket (top), Italian, 2nd half of the 19th century. A gold and Roman mosaic pendant in the form of a bulla *with a representation of the lion of St. Mark (centre). A gold, ruby and baroque pearl pendant (bottom) set with a sardonyx cameo of the Judgement of Paris, probably by Castellani.*

It used to be said that a Victorian jewellery fashion lasted just long enough for the lady of the house to find her maid wearing a one-and-sixpenny version of it. This is a simplification: some styles were evergreen and never out of fashion for long; others were so crazy or tasteless that they did not survive the season. Between these two extremes many fashions came and went. Certainly in this age of prosperity and social change more people were wearing jewellery than ever before and they were wearing more of it. Trends may be caricatured as follows: between 1840 and 1860 romantic, convoluted, grotesque, flamboyant; between 1860 and 1880 mechanistic, experimental, innovative, visual; between 1880 and 1900 subtle, elegant, witty, personal. Throughout the whole period fashions were colourful, eclectic, eccentric, sentimental and sometimes morbid.

To some degree the 1830s represent a transition from the post-Napoleonic period. By the end of the decade grandiose parures and matched pairs of bracelets were on their way out, the frothy cannetille settings replaced by voluptuous stamped scrollwork, the pastel shades of aquamarine and pink topaz extinguished by the full-blooded colours of carbuncle and turquoise. Enamel was often *en plein* – flooded all over the surface of a jewel.

By the time Victoria came to the throne in 1837 the whole mood of jewellery had changed: it was no longer neutral, a mere adjunct to the costume, but frankly romantic, a statement, a challenge even, demanding a response. An early Victorian woman of fashion wore golden serpents round her neck and wrist; a long neck chain fastened with a tiny beringed hand swayed at her waist; a jewel glimmered on her forehead; her earrings hung half-way to the shoulder. Designs were consciously elaborate, perhaps faintly perverse – rotten branches entwined like supple twigs or ribbons tangled in irresolvable knots. Gold was often "coloured" or given a matt finish and smothered with engraved decoration, imparting to it the appearance of having been eaten away by time.

Jewellers began looking to the past, not learning from it as yet but borrowing from its architecture, a baroque cartouche here, a Gothic ogive there. From now on fashions in jewellery became much more sensitive to world events, and books, the theatre, archaeological discoveries, military campaigns, indeed anything that might be called "news", stood a strong chance of being immortalized in personal ornament.

The Romantic and nationalistic feeling which swept through Europe in the 19th century gave rise to an Indian summer of European folk art, fuelled by increased earnings from the land, in which the relationship between city and peasant jewellery was never more complex. Country styles were borrowed by city jewellers and vice versa. This preoccupation with folk costume and ornament was apparent right through the century and was later to influence the Arts

and Crafts Movement.

In the 1850s there was no abrupt change of direction in jewellery fashions. Gothic and particularly baroque designs were just as plentiful although they seem to have been tighter and more formal in interpretation. Simple strap-and-buckle bracelets became popular. *Champlevé* enamel was conspicuous in white and two shades of blue; less so were the purplish almandine garnets and lemon-yellow chrysolites.

Jewellery design is related to other fashions, particularly hairstyles. When the hair covers the ears, as it did in the styles of the 1850s, there is less scope for interesting earring design, and this period saw the temporary eclipse of the earring. In the 1860s, however, the chignon appeared: the hair was now pulled back and fastened with a jewelled comb, exposing the ears. Jewellers made up for lost time and earrings were made in a profusion of styles and designs, although always of the pendent variety. In fact, in the early part of the decade, the whole approach to jewellery changed and the emphasis shifted away from content to technique and effect. The mid-Victorian com-

In spite of the growth of mass production and the demands of the market, skilled craftsmanship still played a very important role in the jewellery trade. Some processes like setting diamonds required a high degree of manual skill and art jewellery was invariably made by hand. Here we see men working at benches with sheepskins slung below them to catch the "lemel", or filings of precious metal. In the foreground of the upper illustration wire is being made at a drawbench, while lower left a craftsman is polishing what appears to be a necklace. Apart from the gaslighting, a modern workshop does not look very different.

mercial jeweller's first intention seems to have been to create a purely visual effect with patterns of light and movement, cunning arrangements of pendent drops, and reflections which subtly echoed and distorted the design. He was now prepared to explore the character of the metal without stifling it with decoration or aggravating it into unnatural shapes. The lapidary took an equally experimental approach, making the stones fit the design in a way which might once have seemed cavalier. Jewellery shapes were now clean and formal: some had a disturbingly mechanistic quality like a valve or a coupling; others incorporated ideas of classical origin.

The Industrial Revolution and the Art Jeweller

It was in this period that the jewellery manufacturer tooled up for mass production. Jewels had been made by multiple production methods since ancient times, either by casting or stamping, the latter being commonplace in the first part of the 19th century. But now machines formerly powered by hand or water were turning over to gas or steam and the pace and scope of

jewellery production were vastly increased. Competition between the many firms of manufacturers was savage, resulting in a continual search for novelties and a lowering of standards in both materials and workmanship. The principal jewellery-making centres of the West where this was happening were the towns of Pforzheim in Germany, Birmingham in England, Providence in Rhode Island, USA, and Gablonz in Bohemia.

However, while the Industrial Revolution was encroaching more and more on the world of the skilled craftsman, a new breed, the art jeweller, was emerging in Italy. Neapolitan jewellers Carlo Giuliano (1831–1895) and Giacinto Mellilo (1845-1915), and especially the Roman Fortunato Pio Castellani (1794–1865), created jewels of small intrinsic value but extraordinary beauty which established the Greek and Etruscan style as the most influential of the period. Some of their jewels were precise copies of Greek or Etruscan originals, others were more in the nature of pastiches. These jewellers were genuinely trying to learn from the past, using it as a repository of ideas and knowledge rather than a box of design tricks.

INTRODUCTION

Castellani, the leading light in this revivalist movement, realized that the ancient Greeks and Etruscans could do things that were beyond his skill and set about trying to rediscover their secrets. The Giuliano family, who came to work in London, moved towards the Italian Renaissance as a source of inspiration and their achievement was to express the spirit of the late 19th century in its eloquent language.

But perhaps more important than the jewels made by the Italians was the change in attitude which they

A gold, sapphire, diamond and enamel bracelet.

heralded. We are beginning to see the first stirrings of an industrial counter-revolution: from 1860 onwards there was a growing reaction against the machine, its effects on people's lives, and the soulless quality of the things it produced. Disillusioned with much of what was on offer, many women of the intelligentsia simply got off the round-about of fashion and either wore no jewellery at all or else went ethnic with peasant jewellery. Others patronized the art jewellers like Giuliano and Castellani, who thought of their work as a vocation rather than a trade.

In Paris at this time there was a renaissance in the art of enamelling, and in the second half of the century techniques which had long fallen into disuse were successfully revived. The exquisite *plique à jour* was rediscovered and Riffaut (1832–1872) made a series of jewels in this magical technique for Frédéric Boucheron, the great impresario of Parisian jewellery. His experiments were of great importance to Lalique and the Art Nouveau jewellers of the 1890s. René Lalique himself (1860–1945) also made jewels in *basse taille*. Lucien Falize travelled to Japan, newly opened to the West, to learn the art of cloisonné. Without exception, all of the great techniques of enamelling on metal were thriving in the French capital at this time.

The Diamond Workers

In the highly specialized jewellery business the workers in diamonds, both cutters and setters, were and are distinct from the rest of the trade. In this field

there was nothing to be learned from the past and new ground was being broken all the time. Diamonds certainly became more plentiful in the 19th century. In the 18th and early 19th centuries Brazil was the primary producer, reaching a peak in the mid-1800s after the discovery of the Bahia fields in 1844. Diamond jewellery at this time was very magnificent in designs of scrolls, ribbons and, above all, flowers.

Since the 18th century jewellers had been trying to imitate flowers and plants in precious metals and diamonds. As their techniques improved the results became less stylized and more naturalistic. They had already learned how to mount a flower *en tremblant* on a spiral spring so that it quivered with the wearer's movements. Settings became lighter and less obtrusive. The naturalistic style reached its apotheosis in the work of a jeweller working in Paris. Oliver Massin (born 1829, retired 1892) invented a method of making the plant stem in tubular sections so that it could be threaded on a length of spring steel, a more natural way of achieving the *tremblant* effect. For the diamond setter the introduction of platinum at the end of the 19th century meant an important change. The great mechanical strength of platinum now enabled him to make mounts that were almost invisible once the stones were set. Another change in the diamonds world was brought about by the arrival of stones from South Africa in 1870. Until then brilliants had been left square and deep, conforming to the shape of the natural crystal, but now that there was such a plentiful supply of diamonds from the Cape the gem could be cut round and shallow, which was extravagant of material but made for a brighter stone.

The diamond jewellery made between the closing years of the 19th century and the outbreak of the First World War has probably never been matched in any period. There was a distinctive 18th-century flavour about many of these jewels and 18th-century styles with their rococo scrolls and latticed backgrounds were in evidence. Just as popular were the Victorian perennials, stars, Maltese crosses and crescents, which were being advertised for sale by jewellers at least as late as 1906.

In the 19th century, where the explorer went, the prospector followed, leading to discoveries of precious minerals, some of them new to science. The enchanting green demantoid garnet was unknown until the 1860s, when specimens were found in Siberia. Crocidolite, or tiger's eye, a golden-brown gem with a satiny sheen, was discovered in large deposits in South West Africa. Black opal was found on Lightning Ridge, Queensland, superb sapphires in Kashmir – until then they had been used as gunflints. The Burmese ruby mines were exploited commercially. Gold was discovered in California, Australia and South Africa. As a result of these discoveries, we are left now with large quantities of 19th-century jewellery: the new abundance of raw materials not only kept the workshops well supplied but also removed much of the need to melt down old jewels to make new.

Mourning Jewellery

Certain kinds of Victorian jewellery reflected the sentimentality of the age. Many jewels were fitted with tiny crystal compartments to contain locks of hair, and sentimental inscriptions abound. "Mizpah" is a fairly common one and signifies "The Lord watch between me and thee when we are absent one from another". An anchor, a cross and a heart on a jewel represent the virtues of Faith, Hope and Charity. The practice of wearing mourning jewellery was already well established and in the 1840s the enamelled cartouches set with crystal hair compartments and rings with forget-me-nots and pearls for tears, charming jewels in their own right, still retained something of the wistful quality of mourning jewellery of the late 18th century. As time went on and mourning rituals became more prescribed and demanding, the market for this jewellery increased until its manufacture assumed the proportions of an industry.

Mourning jewellery was made in a variety of materials which could be of "any colour so long as it was black": enamel, jet, onyx, glass, Berlin cast iron, papier mâché, vulcanite (an early form of plastic) and petrified oak from the Irish bogs. Most included a lock of the dead person's hair preserved under a little window and a brief epitaph with the appropriate names and dates. Later designs were formal and chilly, expressing awfulness and finality rather than sadness and regret. The dour and dreadful figure of Victoria grieving for her lost Albert had a lot to answer for, but as her influence waned in the more relaxed atmosphere of the Belle Epoque mourning jewellery was less in evidence.

Belle Epoque

The influence of Edward and his enchanting Danish bride Alexandra was felt long before they came to the throne. They encouraged fashions that were exuberant but disciplined, gay but not wanton. Shapes became more fluent, colours softer under the influence of Art Nouveau. Coloured stones of every kind were worn, especially the more exotic varieties – alexandrite, demantoid garnet and cat's eye. The leek-green peridot was said to be the favourite stone of the Prince of Wales. Alexandra was seen to like mauve so amethysts were fashionable. But without doubt it was the diamond and the pearl which held pride of place. Pearls were worn either as a long *sautoir* or close to the throat in several short strings as a *collier de chien*; curiously shaped baroque pearls from the Mississippi freshwater mussel were hung as pendants from many semiprecious jewels.

A gold and enamel buckle designed by Chardon and made by Le Turcq for Boucheron in 1903.

INFLUENCES

1

2

The Renaissance may be counted, along with Gothic and Classical Greek, among the most important historical influences to shape Victorian jewellery fashions. It appeared in different interpretations; motifs were often lifted from architecture – caryatids, cartouches and strapwork – and composed in ornaments which, although very effective, bore no resemblence to Renaissance jewellery. The intricate strapwork and figures in this early 17th-century oak panel (1), carved in relief, painted and gilded, are echoed in a lavishly executed necklace and brooch (2), c. 1860. Fashioned in the French Neo-Renaissance style by Rodolphi, a Danish jeweller working in Paris in the middle of the 19th century, it is in enamelled gold set with emeralds, rubies, diamonds, and hung with pearls The Renaissance motifs are repeated in the putto and satyr which crown both the brooch and the necklace, a detail of which is shown right.

La funicolare del Vesuvio.

3

4

MIDLAND
RAILWAY

Cook's EASTER HOLIDAY EXCURSION
TO
SCOTLAND.

ON THURSDAY, APRIL 9TH
FOR 5 or 9 DAYS,

From BRISTOL, Clifton Down, Redland, Montpelier, BATH, Gloucester, Cheltenham,
Worcester, Malvern, Evesham, Alcester, and Redditch (to certain Stations), BIRMINGHAM,
WOLVERHAMPTON, WALSALL, Tamworth, Burton, and DERBY, to

EDINBURGH, GLASGOW
CARLISLE, DUMFRIES, CASTLE DOUGLAS,
Kirkcudbright, Greenock, Ayr
KILMARNOCK, STIRLING, PERTH,
DUNDEE, ARBROATH, FORFAR, BRECHIN,
MONTROSE, STONEHAVEN.
ABERDEEN, INVERNESS, &c.

THIRD CLASS RETURN TICKETS
Will also be issued by these trains, to return any day within 16 Days from date of issue.
For Times, Fares, Conditions, etc., see Small Bills.

For Tickets and further particulars of above, and of Tourist and Excursion Arrangements in SCOTLAND, see Programmes to be obtained at the Booking Offices of
the MIDLAND RAILWAY COMPANY, or at the Offices of

Thos. COOK & Son,
Originators of the European Excursion and Tourist System—Established 1841.

JOHN MATHIESON, General Manager.

Derby, March, 1903.
Thos. Cook & Son, Printers, London and Birmingham.

5

6

Whenever the Victorian tourist went in search of ruins or mountains, jewellers busied themselves making souvenirs. In Italy, the romantic traveller scaled Vesuvius on the funicular railway (3) and brought back cameos carved from Vesuvian lava, (this one, 4, set in gold, c. 1850-80), mosaics from Rome and Florence, and coral from Naples and Genoa.

Thomas Cook (5) exploited the fashion set by the Queen for everything Scottish and astute Scots devised a variety of pieces to tempt the traveller: jewels set with grouse claws, granite, freshwater pearls, and above all, polished agates and jaspers from the surrounding hills, and known as Scotch pebble jewellery. The Scotch pebble bracelet and brooches (6) are set in silver, the central one in the shape of a Scottish dirk.

These gold and turquoise pendent earrings (1) of c. 1840 are built up from elements of stamped sheet metal. Although large, the earrings are hollow and so light in weight.

1

2

The rococo design and elaborately festooned chains of this gold and pink topaz brooch (2) are typically mid 19th century, as is the top of the carbuncle and diamond pendant (3) (c. 1855), which forms a coulant designed to slide freely on the tubular chain. The buxom curves and plushy colour of the carbuncles are set off by the sparkle and delicacy of the diamond foliage which also helps to hold the two big cabochons in place. The oatgrain-shaped diamond drops are characteristic of the period.

3

4

A gold and enamel bracelet based on Gothic architecture, probably French, c. 1845 (4).

5

6

The scrollwork on the gold and turquoise cartouche-shaped brooch (5) contrasts well with the matt ground. In the mid-19th century brooches tended to be designed along the horizontal axis. This is a machine-made piece of good quality; c. 1840. In the garnet and diamond demi-parure (6) the substantial pavé-set

diamond scrollwork is kept clear of the garnets which are held in place with a "cut-down" setting, that is a rim of gold filed to a bevel but with small points of metal left to buttress it. The design, engineering, and the presence of a pair of earrings indicate a date in the 1840s.

THE ART JEWELLERS

*This necklace and pair of matching pendants (**1**) are possibly from a diadem. Finely decorated with filigree and granulation, the pendants are embossed with Thetis riding a sea monster and carrying the armour of Achilles. These jewels were made by Castellani in around 1870, after Greek originals excavated at Kul Oba in southern Russia in 1864.*

1

2

*The gold headband in gold and champlevé enamel set with a ruby and turquoises (**2**) was designed by A. W. N. Pugin (1812–52) in the Gothic style and made by John Hardman and Co. in 1848. Pugin was the first designer to reject the machine and advocate a return to hand craftsmanship and therefore foreshadowed the Arts and Crafts movement. Regrettably he designed very little jewellery.*

*A gold, cabochon ruby and pearl pendant (**3**) by Giuliano in their own distinctive interpretation of the Renaissance style. The Giuliano family often used black and white enamel in this way, to tone down rather than enhance the colour-scheme of a jewel.*

3

4

This necklace of gold and diamonds (4) is set with painted enamels of nymphs and cupids in "Pompeian" style and is by Eugène Fontenay (1823–87), the leading exponent in France of the Greek Revivalist style: the drop-shaped pendants and butterflies have apparently been borrowed from Greek and Etruscan jewellery.

BOUCHERON

Frédéric Boucheron opened his first shop in Paris in the Place du Palais Royal in 1858. From the outset he showed an extraordinary intuitive response to the tastes and fashions of his time. There was scarcely a style or a new technique in which he was not intimately concerned if he was not its actual instigator. He was showing *plique à jour* enamel, which years later was to become *synonymous* with Art Nouveau, at the Paris Exhibition of 1867, while Lalique was still a child. The Mogul emperors retained lapidaries skilled enough to engrave diamond, the hardest substance known – so did Boucheron. Like Benvenuto Cellini he made jewels of chiselled steel.

Boucheron was a keen observer of nature and brought something greater than realism to the translation of living plants into jewels, selecting not merely the conventional roses and marigolds, but hedgerow thistles and spectacular twigs of plane tree leaves. His jewellery typified everything the American travelling millionaire was looking for in late 19th-century Europe. It was daring, original, chic, and of superb quality in both materials and workmanship. The firm moved to the Place Vendôme in 1893. A branch was opened in Moscow in 1902, but Frédéric did not live to see the firm established in London and New York in the following year. He was succeeded by his son Louis.

A pair of hair ornaments in plique à jour *enamel, diamonds and pearls, made by Riffault,* c. *1870, for Boucheron.*

MID-CENTURY WORK

This 1870s bracelet of coloured golds (**1**) is inlaid in a diapered pattern and set with turquoise. Chequered patterns and variations on them were popular after the Great Exhibition of 1852. The smooth finish and massive appearance are characteristically mid-Victorian. The gold and Florentine mosaic brooch (**2**) has a mosaic inlay of white shell and malachite on a ground of black marble and dates from c. 1860.

1

2

(**3**) At the top, a gold, turquoise, enamel and half-pearl demi-parure of 1870. The necklace, with its festoons of "brazilian" chain and fringed pendants, illustrates a basic theme which appeared in numerous variations, often with a classical Greek flavour, throughout the 1860s and after. The circular form of the brooch is also typical as is the broad hinged bracelet. To the left is a gold and turquoise padlock. Lock and key jewels are eternal and universal; for example, in the Far East they are worn to preserve life by locking in the soul while in the West they are tokens of love. This example was probably a bracelet fastening. Below, a gold and carbuncle bracelet of 1860 in a very simple Gothic design; and bottom, a gold necklace in classical Greek style from the last 30 years of the 19th century. The small holes pierced in the hollow drops are not purely decorative, but also served to vent expanding gases when they were being soldered.

3

A cameo bracelet of c. 1880 made of gold and sardonyx (**5**). Sardonyx is a type of agate formed in alternate layers of flesh pink and white. To cut a cameo the stone is orientated so that the layers run parallel to the surface. The design is cut in the white so that the flesh-coloured background is exposed. In this case the stone has been worked in three layers and is set in a border of flowers and doves. In the gold and shell cameo demi-parure (**6**) the cameos have been cut from a conch shell, which resembles sardonyx in that it has a stratified structure with a pale outer layer and a flesh-coloured lining. Being softer than sardonyx, it is easier to work which makes it less durable, but it is cheaper. The back of a sardonyx usually reveals the concavity of a sea shell. Jewels of the design illustrated have been made for the tourist trade from 1860 to the present.

The stones of the gold and malachite parure (**4**) are cut in unconventional shapes and applied with a mechanistic quadrant and rivet-head design.

MOURNING JEWELLERY

The mount of this gold mourning locket (**1**) set with black onyx applied with a rose diamond and freshwater pearl star, is engraved and decorated with champlevé enamel.

1

2

3

These designs for mourning rings by John Brogden (**3**) were taken from an album of designs found recently in the jeweller's archive.

A mid 19th-century bracelet of braided hair, (**2**) the clasp set with a hair compartment. The gold mounts have been stamped out by machine. Below, the gold and hair brooch representing an anchor may have signified that the person commemorated was a seafarer, or have been used as a symbol of the Christian faith. To its left, a gold, enamel and hair brooch represents a snake with a heart pendent from its jaws, a favoured early Victorian motif.

The fringe of chain on the gold and black-enamel mourning brooch (**4**) is often seen in jewels of the 1860s. The reverse is dated 1866.

4

MACHINE-MADE JEWELLERY

The garnet necklace (**1**) was made in Gablonz, Bohemia, in the late 19th century. This cheap and effective jewellery was exported all over Europe. The locally mined stones were often cut by children and set in very low carat gold.

1

2

The front and back of the late 19th-century brooch (**2**) would have been stamped out separately and soldered together. The borders and brooch fitting would be added at this stage and the stones set last of all.

4

3

Making the dies for a machine-made jewel is the most expensive part of the process. However, few would be needed to produce this simple bracelet (**3**) which was made in the mid-19th century, probably in central Europe, and relatively little handwork would be required to finish it. This good quality gold brooch (**4**) was made in the 1860s, probably in England, the home of the Industrial Revolution, where a huge amount of jewellery was produced in small backstreet workshops. The incomplete article would be passed from one workshop to another for each stage of the manufacturing process.

NOVELTIES

1

2

A demantoid garnet and diamond bird brooch (**2**). Demantoid garnets were first discovered in Siberia in the Ural mountains, about 1860. Jewels set with these stones which rival the diamond in fire and the peridot in colour were very fashionable in late Victorian and Edwardian times.

The design of this cabochon amethyst and diamond bumble bee brooch (**1**) of c.1890 probably had its origin in the Second Empire since the bee was the emblem of the House of Bonaparte. Winged insects – gadflies, dragonflies, butterflies, even houseflies – were very popular in jewellery from 1860.

The carved carbuncle, emerald and rose-diamond beetle brooch (**3**) dates from c.1865. Large and grotesque beetle brooches are usually of French origin.

3

4

5

Butterfly brooches of this type (**4**) were manufactured in large numbers at the turn of the century. This is an inexpensive little jewel set with rose diamonds and coloured stones. Small brooches were worn several at a time and in 1907 they helped to anchor the masses of lace which cascaded down the corsage.

A demantoid garnet and diamond lizard brooch (**5**). Both frog and lizard brooches set with these gems were popular around 1900. The frog was a universal symbol of love while the natural colour of the lizard makes it an ideal vehicle for the fashionable demantoid garnet.

The decoration of this enamel and half-pearl heart pendant (**6**) made c.1900 is derived from the 18th century, although in the original the enamel would probably have been blue rather than green. The brooch (**7**) representing a "merrythought" or wishbone uses the cockerel motif, following the success of Emile Rostand's comedy Chanticleer. *It is also the national emblem of France. The cock wards off bad luck because its cry scares away the evil forces of the night.*

6

7

8

9

A heart-shaped diamond locket (**8**). The ribbon bow which forms the surmount appears in many jewels made in the latter part of the century. The enamelled cufflinks (**9**) represent the pleasures of youth and typify the frivolity of fin de siècle.

11

10

A ruby and diamond monkey brooch (**10**) of c.1880. Popular literature and art of the late 19th and early 20th centuries were preoccupied with the notion of man's evolution through the ages.

A gold brooch (**11**) representing a pair of lovebirds perched on a coral branch dating from the last quarter of the 19th century.

(*1*) The naturalism of the three ribbon-bow brooches and the Alexandra rose is typical of the Belle Epoque and in vivid contrast with the more formal Victorian star, cross, and target designs. All, however, are long-standing favourites, returning to fashion time and again in one form or another. There would be little difference between this very English Maltese cross and one made three quarters of a century earlier.

The diamond aigrette (*3*) was designed to be worn in the hair with an osprey – a plume of egret feathers. This style was introduced in the 1890s but persisted in one form or another until well after the First World War. Winged hair ornaments are said to have been popularized by Boucheron, and this was also a time when Western man was obsessed with the idea of flight.

3

2

4

5

6

The gold and diamond scrollwork of this pearl and diamond pendant (*2*) enclosed in a somewhat architectural border hint at a European rather than an English origin and suggest a date in the last quarter of the 19th century.

In the years before the First World War, rings were worn in considerable numbers, sometimes one or more on each finger. This boat-shaped marquise ring (*4*) is typical of the period, and (*5*) also dates from this time.

Swags, garlands and ribbon bows are characteristic of the Belle Epoque. As the style moved on into the 20th century designs became more stylized; this charming corsage ornament (*6*) dates from just before the First World War.

DIAMONDS

1

2

This diamond stomacher brooch
(1) has a scroll design sprigged
with foliage and is surmounted by
a spray of collet-set diamonds
mounted on knife wires; it dates
from the last quarter of the 19th
century.

Designs for diamond jewellery
by Watherston and Brogden (2).
The stars (top left and right) are
designed to be worn either singly
as suites of brooches or screwed on
to a frame as a tiara. The sea-horse
brooch (top centre) is very
uncommon, but diamond owls
are met with from time to time. The
rest – the rivière necklace, the
crosses, half-hoop bracelets,
butterfly brooches, flower sprays,
horseshoes, etc – are all
representative of a first class late
Victorian London jeweller's
stock-in-trade.

*The idea of the bow brooch
arises directly out of the costume
and blends very closely with it
when worn. This illustration (3)
shows a corsage ornament in
which the connection is carried to
its logical conclusion. The lace of
the bow is of blackened platinum
sprigged with diamond flowers
and with an edging of gold and
diamonds. This construction is not
only decorative but very light in
wear. Made by Lefort for
Boucheron in 1908.*

3

4

6

5

*The crescent is perhaps the oldest
of jewel designs. This simple theme
exists in many variants, two of
which are illustrated (4 and 5).
Most of those made in the last
quarter of the 19th century are
primarily brooches, but were
provided with a pronged fitting
which allowed them also to be
worn in the hair "à la Diane". This
diamond spray brooch is a design
of wild anemones (6) from the mid
19th century.*

BELLE EPOQUE

A peridot and diamond pendant brooch (*1*) in a design of garlanded ribbons and flowers, c.1890. The leek-green peridot was said to have been the favourite stone of Edward, Prince of Wales. The quiet tints and subtle effects of semi-precious stones like aquamarine, cat's eye, alexandrite, moonstone and the Australian and Mexican opal were very appropriate to the light, open designs of this time. Half-hoop bracelet designs proliferated from 1870 onwards. The simple theme of a hinged and clasped hoop with the decoration confined to the front lent itself to many variations, some quite elaborate. The illustration (*2*) shows cluster, foliate and entrelac de rubans designs. The crossover, fourth from the left, was very popular.

1

QUEEN ALEXANDRA

The combined influence of Edward VII and his beautiful Danish bride Alexandra was felt long before the couple came to the throne. Two jewellery styles co-existed at that time: Victorian, which was formal and impressive, and Edwardian, which had a more cosmopolitan flavour. Alexandra herself was a woman of simple tastes, content to wear no ornament other than a single rose in the daytime. State occasions required her to dress for the part, however, and she did so with dignity and flair. Round her neck she customarily wore a close-fitting *collier de chien*, a fashion she is said to have

Queen Alexandra dressed for a state occasion.

adopted to conceal a small scar on her throat.

She favoured a tiara in the imperial Russian style, the design of which was based on a peasant head-dress, the *kokoshnik*. When Alexandra came to the throne jewellery was worn more creatively to suit the age and looks of the wearer: here she wears the tiara perched on top of a mass of curls. This new freedom had its limits. At dinner Edward was once heard to say to a lady guest, "The Princess has taken the trouble to wear a tiara – why haven't you?"

A necklace (*3*) reputed to have once belonged to Queen Alexandra. The hexagonal outlines of the amethysts blend more readily with the diamond scrollwork than would more conventional circular shapes. This regal jewel is saved from being overwhelming by the pendent garlands and undulating scrollwork which also give it an 18th-century flavour. The Queen often wore amethysts, said to be her favourite stones.

A pearl and diamond necklace dating from the last half of the 19th century. This jewel may also be adapted for wear as a tiara.

A late 19th-century diamond crescent brooch.

Pendant of silver-gilt and plique-à-jour enamel with three baroque pearl blossoms. German or Austrian, c. 1900-10.

CHAPTER SIX

JEWELLERY FOR AESTHETES

INTRODUCTION

Maison Vever, one of Paris's best-known joailliers in the Art Nouveau period, produced the stunning pendant–brooch and necklace. The works of the brothers Paul and Henri Vever were more restrained and controlled than those of their admired contemporary René Lalique, but nonetheless bore similar motifs and were as expertly executed. Of enamelled gold, diamonds and sapphires, the pendant features two facing peacocks, their feet centred on a large pearl. The peacock was a popular Art Nouveau subject, its showy plumage often represented in jewellery, glass, fabric, etc.

The quarter-century or so leading up to the year 1900 embraced on the one hand the waning of the Victorian era and on the other the onset of the modern age. The Industrial Revolution rumbled on; electricity and photography were nascent sciences; innovative technologies were bursting upon an advancing Western world – and the first fine art to be called "modern" (by later art historians) was being created by Manet, Cézanne, Monet and their contemporaries.

In the decorative arts, too, signs of a new age were beginning to reveal themselves, in techniques, materials, themes, influences and purpose, and jewellery was one of the most visible and exciting of the plastic arts to display these signs in, appropriately enough, the vocabulary of the turn-of-the-century Art Nouveau ("New Art") style. Art Nouveau was a French design movement characterized by whiplash curves, references to nature and virtuoso techniques; and nowhere was this better seen than in goldsmiths' work, notably the jewels of René Lalique, the Maison Vever and Georges Fouquet. Gallic Art Nouveau made waves throughout all of Europe and the Americas, but so too did the Jugendstil ("Young Style") jewels of Germany, the decidedly modernist works of Austria's Wiener Werkstätte and the vast related output of American and other European designers, some anonymous, others well known. Designers of the hand-crafted and mass-produced jewellery of Great Britain, including that of Liberty & Co. and the Glasgow School, shared an aesthetic, a design philosophy and working methods of the German and Austrian jewellers and were linked by their use of materials.

The Arts and Crafts Designers

The Arts and Crafts Movement is generally considered as one which looked back, rather than ahead, for its inspiration and guiding principles. The movement, whose leading exponents were the critic John Ruskin and the multi-talented designer–writer–activist William Morris, was essentially a reaction against the encroaching modern age, against the squalor and ills that were perceived to have been brought on by industrialization, against the shoddy, machine-made products that were being spewed forth. Arts and Crafts designs –interiors, architecture, furniture, books, metalwork and jewellery – signalled a romantic, though not rigid, return to earlier, purer aesthetics and techniques; their creators took their inspiration largely from what they viewed as the simple, unsullied Middle Ages – its cathedrals, furnishings, even costumes, and perhaps, most significantly, its workers' guilds and their guiding rules and methods.

The finest Arts and Crafts pieces are one-off, appreciated not for their value or their weight, but for their design, their colour, their workmanship. Unlike most French or Belgian Art Nouveau pieces, the Arts and Crafts designs tended to

be simple, even somewhat primitive, figural or floral motifs, or more complex, interlaced (*entrelac*) or knotted patterns of Celtic inspiration. This latter type of design was best shown off on myriad belt or waist buckles and clasps by designers like Oliver Baker, Archibald Knox, Kate Fisher, Kate Allen, and Edgar Simpson (many of them sold at Liberty). For the stone-set pieces – which included brooches, pendants, bracelets, necklaces, hatpins and of course rings – such polished stones as turquoise, amethyst, opal, lapis lazuli and rose quartz were set into silver or gold with tiny open circles, beaded clusters or florets often forming a frame around them.

Archibald Knox (1864–1953) was born, studied and taught on the Isle of Man until 1897, when he moved to London to lecture at three of its art colleges; by 1899 he was employed by Liberty & Co., designing an extensive array (over 400 pieces) of exquisite enamelled or stone-set silver and gold jewellery (as well as silver and pewter objects in the "Cymric" and "Tudric" lines respectively) and eventually becoming their chief designer. His teaching and design speciality was Celtic ornament, and his distinctively smooth and usually symmetrically curving, interlaced patterns obviously derived from medieval Celtic stonework and illuminated manuscripts.

C.R. Ashbee (1863–1942) was an architect as well as a silver and jewellery designer. Probably his best-known creation was the Guild and School of Handicraft, which he founded in 1888 and which, although shortlived, was distinguished for its furniture, metalwork and, above all, for its jewellery. Ashbee himself provided a great many of the designs, which included the peacock, delicate flowers and a tiny sailing ship, the so-called "craft of the guild". Among the jewellery designers who were a part of the guild were Fred T. Partridge, whose exquisitely crafted works, especially his combs, echo French Art Nouveau jewels, and his use of such materials as brass, shell, horn and steel also reveal a kinship with his Gallic contemporaries. Partridge married May Hart, an enamellist of great skill whose use of the *plique-à-jour* technique, though not as elaborate as that of the European jewellers, was nevertheless expert and resulted in lovely pieces.

Another important English guild, the Artificers' Guild, was founded in 1901 by Nelson Dawson (1859–1942) in Chiswick in London and was taken over two years later by Montague Fordham, erstwhile director of the Birmingham Guild of Handicraft. Along with his wife, Edith, Dawson created beautiful enamelled jewellery, often decorated with floral and avian motifs. Dawson had learned the skill of enamelling from Alexander Fisher, who was known for his plaques, sconces, and other large decorated pieces composed of layers of enamel on a foil ground.

Like many Arts and Crafts jewellers, another husband and wife team, Arthur and Georgina Gaskin, were connected to the city of Birmingham. Their inspirations and output were various – the former ranged from Italian Renaissance to Scandinavian folk art – and their pieces, whether a busily organic brooch with tiny enamelled florets or a simple silver necklace pendant with green chrysoprase hearts, were all expertly crafted by hand.

Henry Wilson (1864–1934), like many other Arts and Crafts designers, initially studied and practised architecture. He produced some exquisite pieces of jewellery at the turn of the century, inspired primarily by nature and the medieval and Renaissance past, and some extraordinary jewels, like earlier Italian masterworks, would feature stunning designs on both front and back.

Omar Ramsden (1873–1939) and Alwyn C.E. Carr (1872–1940) produced jewellery with religious overtones (this in addition to their more numerous metal ceremonial objects), and another significant teacher-designer-jewellery maker was Harold Stabler (1872–1945), much of whose cloisonné enamelwork, was made in collaboration with his wife, Phoebe, in his Hammersmith studio. Oliver Baker (1859–1939) and Jessie M. King (1875–1949) were two jewellery designers working for Liberty. Baker dis-

tinguished himself for his handsome silver buckle designs, usually hammered, with strong *entrelac* or curling motifs, and embellished with cabochons of semi-precious stones. King's Liberty jewels tend to betray their Glaswegian origins, especially her lovely enamelled-silver belt buckles whose florets nearly camouflage Charles Rennie Mackintosh-inspired birds amid their trelliswork.

Unlike objects in other fields, such as furniture, metalwork and pottery, fine American Arts and Crafts

The enamelled-silver belt buckle dates from the turn of the century and was made by Nelson and Edith Dawson. Floral motifs abounded on the Dawsons' hand-crafted pieces, whose surface and textures were purposefully matt and grainy, which gave them a quiet, gentle beauty. Nelson Dawson was the founder of the Artificers' Guild, established in Chiswick in 1901.

jewellery was a rarity; the Gallic Art Nouveau style seemed the greater influence on American jewellers, who in the main were companies rather than guilds or individual craftsmen. However, one firm, Marcus & Co., created some exquisite Arts and Crafts-style (or "crafts revival") jewellery in addition to Art Nouveau, and Florence Koehler, working in Chicago, fashioned pieces akin to those of her British contemporaries.

France, Belgium and the United States

The Arts and Crafts Movement itself, as directly connected to Morris, was all but dead by the early 20th century. As its part in the decorative arts in Britain decreased, Art Nouveau was emerging, with all its waves and tendrils, *femmes fatales* and comely maidens, botanical verity and Symbolist allusions. There was the hyper-organic furniture and ironwork of Hector Guimard, the homage-to-nature glass and wood of Emile Gallé and Louis Majorelle, but most of all the exquisitely crafted, often dazzlingly pictorial goldsmith's work of René Lalique, Georges Fouquet, Lucien Gaillard and other Parisian jewellers. Their acclaim was worldwide, their clients –such as actress Sarah Bernhardt and courtesan Liane de Pougy – world famous, and their influence permanent.

Unlike the subdued forms of Arts and Crafts jewellery, Art Nouveau jewellery could be dramatic, symbolic, ostentatious and, in the case of some of Lalique's massive chest ornaments, impractically overwhelming in size, weight and impact. The types of jewellery worn ranged from diadems and combs, necklaces and pendants to shoe buckles, bracelets, stickpins and rings, and the colours, materials and techniques were wildly diverse: there were precious, semiprecious and non-precious gems and metals, substances like glass, horn and tortoiseshell, and expert enamelling of the translucent, opalescent, *champlevé,* cloisonné and *plique-à-jour* varieties.

Without doubt, Frenchman René Lalique (1860–1945) was the master goldsmith of the Art Nouveau era. His one-off, exquisitely crafted rings, bracelets, dog-collars (decorative central plaques usually attached to ribbons or rows of pearls, and worn tightly across the neck), brooches, hair-combs, necklaces and tiaras were truly works of art, widely praised and exhibited in Europe and abroad, and,

inevitably, imitated in varying degrees of quality and imagination in France and elsewhere. Lalique's innovative joining of "lesser" materials with precious gems and metals, as well as his rich use of natural, fantastic, literary, Neo-classical, oriental, Symbolist and even religious images, combine to make his body of jewels a significant contribution to the art of the goldsmith, and to the decorative arts in general.

Although overshadowed by Lalique's highly imaginative, original and widely varied designs, the goldsmith's work of several other Frenchmen in the Art Nouveau period ranks among the finest decorative work of that time: the Maison Vever (headed by the brothers, Paul and Henri, and employing such notable figures as the engraver Lucien Gautrait and the illustrator Eugène Grasset); Lucien Gaillard, who was much influenced by Japanese style and techniques; Eugène Feuillâtre, a skilled enamellist who had been apprenticed to Lalique; Georges Fouquet, whose firm commissioned Alphonse Mucha to design jewels for Sarah Bernhardt; Edward Colonna, born in Germany and who worked in France and the United States designing jewellery (and furniture) for Samuel Bing's Maison de l'Art Nouveau, as did Bing's son, Marcel; and Jules Desbois, whose chased-gold and silver brooches, buckles and buttons usually featured languorous female nudes or profiled faces in detailed bas-relief.

Numerous established jewellery firms, such as Boucheron, and newly founded retail companies like Julius Meier-Graefe's La Maison Moderne, produced handsome Art Nouveau pendants, brooches, combs and so on. The young Paul Follot and Maurice Dufrêne both designed heavily florid pieces for Meier-Graefe's Paris shop, and Théodore Lambert designed rather subdued floral and foliate pieces which were executed by Paul Templier and featured much openwork and filigree. In Belgium, Philippe Wolfers (1858–1929) designed outstanding goldsmith's work for the family firm, Wolfers Frères.

Across the Atlantic, several American jewellery-producing firms marketed wares highly reminiscent of French Art Nouveau. Foremost among these was the Gorham Corporation, founded in Providence, Rhode Island, in the early 19th century. Although Gorham employed many English designers in the 1800s, its trademarked "Martelé" jewellery, produced from around 1890, was often distinctly Gallic in feel. Unger Bros in Newark, New Jersey, also offered jewellery in the Art Nouveau style, most of it silver, sometimes lightly vermeiled. Other American firms producing Art Nouveau jewellery were Krementz (also in Newark) and Frank M. Whiting Company in North Attleboro, Massachusetts; while countless other costume jewellery firms in America – and Europe – produced pieces influenced by French designs (though often poorly executed by machine).

The maker of this Austrian pendant of c. 1910 is unknown, but it is an interesting Continental jewel featuring a Celtic interlace motif of silver, aquamarine, peridot, chrystoberyl and a baroque pearl. The octagonal pendant may have been designed by a member of the Wiener Werkstätte.

Tiffany & Co. in New York, founded in 1834, produced a small number of outstanding Art Nouveau jewellery pieces under the directorship of Louis Comfort Tiffany (1848–1933), better known for his stained-glass windows, Favrile glass and leaded lamps. The "art jewellery" department was opened in 1902 under the supervision of Julia Munson; Louis Comfort himself designed necklaces, brooches and other pieces, which often combined semiprecious and precious stones with glass or enamel-on-metal. Their style was more Revival or even Byzantine than that of typical Gallic Art Nouveau jewellery.

Moderne Jewellery in Germany and Austria

In Austria, where the *moderne* style took root rather early – in the last years of 19th century and the first decade or so of the 20th – some amazingly far-seeing pieces of jewellery were being designed by the likes of Josef Hoffmann, the architect, and his contemporaries. The Wiener Werkstätte dominated by circles, squares and other geometric shapes; a square-framed Hoffmann brooch of silver, for instance, features a group of lapis lazuli cabochons in circular, square, rectangular and triangular shapes, intermingling with tiny heart-shaped leaves. Jewels such as this were not mass-produced and occupy a significant place in early 20th-century jewellery design – neither Arts and Crafts nor Art Nouveau, but decidedly new and different. However, there were Austrian jewellers whose works distinctly echoed Gallic Art Nouveau, among them Franz Hauptmann and the firm of Rozet & Fischmeister.

Jugendstil ("Young Style") Germany proved a fertile ground for jewellery designers, with a huge output of pieces from, above all, Pforzheim, where the firm of Theodor Fahrner (1868–1928) mass-produced generally inexpensive jewels to the designs of Josef Maria Olbrich, Henry van de Velde, Moritz Gradl, Patriz Huber and other designers allied to the Darmstadt artists' colony set up by the Grand Duke Ernst-Ludwig of Hesse, a supporter of the Arts and Crafts Movement. In other German cities – Munich, Dresden, Berlin – jewellery was being created in a variety of styles, from Lalique-like (by Robert Koch), to Wolfers-inspired (Theodor von Gosen), to distinctively Jugendstil, such as Berliner Hermann Hirzel's leafy gold forms designed by goldsmith Louis Werner.

On the whole, other European countries produced jewellery which either copied mainstream French pieces or adhered to indigenous provincial or unimaginatively traditional-European styles and forms. In Denmark, however, Mogens Ballin, Harald Slott-Müller, Eric Magnussen and above all Georg Jensen distinguished themselves with their handsome designs. Jensen (1866–1935), a silversmith, potter and sculptor, opened a jewellery atelier in Copenhagen in 1904, later producing large silver pieces such as coffeepots and trays in addition to his jewellery. His heavy silver brooches, combs, buckles and bracelets – some highlighted with cabochon amber or other semiprecious stones – featured stylized flowers, leaves, birds and animals.

In Eastern Europe, too, the influence of French and Belgian designers could be seen, most visibly in the Art Nouveau-style goldsmith's work of the esteemed Russian firm of Peter Carl Fabergé. Curvilinear, organic forms adorned many a House of Fabergé bejewelled piece, but this was just one type of decoration they adopted, revival and peasant styles being two others. In Budapest, while the designs of Oskar Huber reflected the more controlled curves of the German jewellers, their flattened *champlevé* enamelwork was akin to traditional, native techniques.

The Pforzheim firm of Theodor Fahrner produced a wide array of jewellery from the late 1800s well into the Art Deco era. Its designs came from both German and English sources, and indeed it made pieces marketed by the London wholesaler Murrle, Bennett & Co. (some with obvious British designs, giving rise to difficulties in their identification today). The lovely enamelled-silver and amethyst necklace was made by Fahrner around 1905.

INFLUENCES

Many English Arts and Crafts
designers were inspired by the
motifs of the Middle Ages. The
Celtic entrelac was often used by
Archibald Knox, who designed the
silver purse frame (**1**), set with
turquoise matrix. Its interlace
patterns are similar to those on the
High Cross of Patrick and
Columba (**2**) at Kells in Ireland,
6th–7th century; and those on the
decorative border of the silver,
gold, copper, and amber- and
glass-studded Ardagh Chalice (**3**),
8th century.

5

French Art Nouveau jewellers adopted imagery from sources as disparate as Symbolist poetry and Oriental prints. René Lalique created the stunning enamelled-gold cock's head diadem (4); the magnificent bird's beak clutches an amethyst. It relates not only to the Utamaro illustration (5), from The Hundred Birds with Humorous Verses, but also to the cloisonné enamelled vase (6), from the Meiji period.

6

Flora and fauna were represented in loving detail by many French Art Nouveau designers – on glass vases, on carved and inlaid furniture and on goldsmith's work. Insects were especially favoured by designers of the Ecole de Nancy: the étagère by Emile Gallé (8), with its monumental dragonfly support, is a superb, even somewhat monstrous, example of this entomological bent. On a smaller scale, René Lalique's delicate pendant (7) of gold, diamonds and plique-à-jour enamel depicts a pair of facing grasshoppers – an exercise in both scientific and symmetrical precision.

7

8

ANIMAL FORMS

From the delicate and everyday, to the monumental and grotesque, the range of creatures depicted on turn-of-the-century jewellery was vast. Even Arts and Crafts designers were not averse to decorating their pieces with the odd avian or other animal motif: the lovely creation (c. 1910) by Arthur and Georgina Gaskin (**1**) incorporates a quartet of tiny birds into its silver and silver-gilt pendant; tourmalines, mother-of-pearl, turquoise and paste set off the metalwork. Another English jewel is the brooch by John Paul Cooper (**2**) comprising a golden stag amid a rock crystal, gold and enamel roundel. The stunning ring tray (**3**) of c. 1900–1 was made by Eugène Feuillâtre, who for a time worked with René Lalique. Four silver serpents make up the frame of the piece, and its central section, of plique-à-jour enamel, features a colourful piscine creature in the Japoniste vein.

1

2

3

René Lalique's large and powerful jewels were often worn by women who were themselves larger than life – such as the actress Sarah Bernhardt and the celebrated dancer and courtesan Liane de Pougy, seen in a photograph of c. 1890–5 wearing a Lalique pendant and head ornament (**4**) The same oxidized-silver, enamel and chrysoprase creation, converted into a brooch, is illustrated alone (**5**). The horrific winged dragon, in the Egyptian taste, was in fact inspired by the Divine Sarah herself, playing the part of Cleopatra.

4

5

6 7

Birds were among the most popular creatures on British Arts and Crafts jewels, and the enamelled-silver, amethyst and peridot ring (**6**), probably by George Hunt, sports a strong avian design. Actually the ring most likely dates from the 1920s, but it is decidedly in the earlier Arts and Crafts mode. The silver and moonstone brooch (**7**) of c. 1910 by the Dane Georg Jensen has a central bird motif. As the moderne style came to dominate his silver, Jensen's animals became more stylized and simplified; this brooch, however, is in his earlier, somewhat heavier, style.

COMBS AND BUCKLES

THE JEWELLERY OF LIBERTY & CO.

In 1875, Arthur Lasenby Liberty (1843–1917) opened a small retail shop in London's Regent Street and called it East India House; he specialized in selling Oriental fabrics and goods, including silks from India and porcelain and screens from Japan. By 1885, the shop had expanded considerably and become extremely popular. Besides importing exotic goods, Liberty was now commissioning English designers to create fabrics, fashions, furniture, pottery and other wares for his shop. At the turn of the century, Liberty & Co. imported, commissioned and sold a huge variety of native, other European and Oriental goods; silver and pewter objects were added to the inventory in the 1890s (sold under the tradenames "Cymric" and "Tudric", respectively), and included a large number of jewellery pieces. Although Liberty insisted on maintaining a policy of anonymity for his designers, his employees — among them Archibald Knox,

Gold, opal and pearl pendant by Archibald Knox for Liberty & Co.

Jessie M. King, Bernard Cuzner, Oliver Baker, Arthur and Georgina Gaskin and Rex Silver — were some of the most prominent names in Arts and Crafts design of the time. The buckles, waist clasps, brooches, pendants, bracelets, rings, necklaces and other Liberty pieces — of smooth or hammered sil-

ver and sometimes gold, highlighted with rich enamelling, moonstones, turquoise, opals, mother-of-pearl, etc. — were distinguished for their innovative designs and colour combinations. The Celtic interlace pattern (attributable to Knox) was perhaps Liberty's best-known motif, but stylized flowers, heart-shaped leaves and loose, sometimes asymmetrical tendrils akin to those of Gallic goldsmith's work were also a part of the vast Liberty repertoire. Besides employing domestic jewellery designers and manufacturers Liberty also bought designs from companies in Pforzheim, Germany, a major jewellery-making centre. Technically, Liberty's factory-made commercial jewels (some with hand-finishing) cannot be deemed Arts and Crafts, as can the hand-crafted creations of the various English artisan guilds, yet so many of their designs, do relate to the spirit of the Arts and Crafts Movement.

Haircombs were a popular accessory at the turn of the century. Some, like the Murrle, Bennett & Co. design (2), were simply shaped, displaying period elements in their added design: here heart-shaped gold leaves alternate with peridots on a tortoiseshell ground.

A long-toothed horn, gold, enamel and opal comb (1) by the Parisian Georges Fouquet, ambitiously carved as evidenced by the openwork motif of stylized lotus blossoms.

1

2

3

4

5

Some of the loveliest Arts and Crafts and Art Nouveau jewels were belt buckles, or clasps for joining together the sides of heavy cloaks that were so often worn at the turn of the century. The handsome silver, plique-à-jour enamel and paste buckle (3); c. 1905, is probably German or Austrian. Its strong, curved design is typically Jugendstil, but its stylized lotus blossoms add a colourful, delicate touch. Joseph Hodel, who was associated with the Bromsgrove Guild of Applied Art in England, designed the silver and chrysoprase buckle (4), with its dense but organized massing of grapes, leaves and encircling tendrils. The chef d'oeuvre (5) by Danish silversmith Georg Jensen dates from c. 1904. Jensen has borrowed a popular motif from his French contemporaries, the dragonfly, and stylized it in his own idiomatic way, using silver, opals and native techniques to produce an arresting, outstanding piece.

MEDIEVAL INFLUENCES

2

Many Arts and Crafts jewellers looked to the Middle Ages (and sometimes the Renaissance) for inspiration regarding materials, techniques and subjects. Two lovely, pictorial pieces are the silver, enamel and garnet brooch (**2**), possibly by the Guild of Handicraft, and the gold, enamel and stone pendant (**1**), by John Paul Cooper. Both these English designs have medieval subjects: a Viking sailing ship and a turreted castle.

1

The substantial belt buckle (**3**) of silver and cloisonné enamel resembles a medieval shield, complete with stylized aquiline motif. Its typical Arts and Crafts border of leaves, grape clusters and tendrils, however, firmly places it in this mode (it is attributed to Harold Stabler, c. 1910). Yet another medievalizing design is the silver and enamel pendant (**5**) by the Englishman Omar Ramsden, c. 1900; its form is like that of a religious triptych, and indeed its central section features a saint bearing shield and sword. Somewhat surprising is René Lalique's wonderful usage of a medieval subject, a couple wearing period headdresses, in a gold, ivory, sapphire, enamel and diamond pendant, c. 1900–2 (**4**).

3

4   5

FIGURATIVE PIECES

1

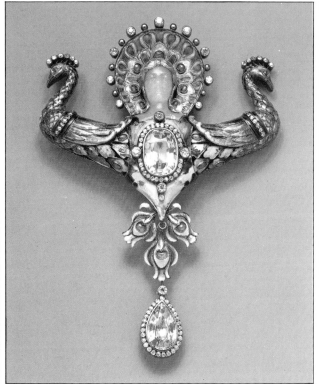

2

Art Nouveau is noted for its depictions of women – usually languorous, long-dressed beauties, but sometimes more sublime, ethereal types, or even femmes fatales. An elaborate bodice adornment (3) features the quintessential Art Nouveau woman; indeed, the gold, enamel, emerald and baroque pearl piece, its figure painted on mother-of-pearl, is a combined effort by the premier illustrator of the time, Czech-born Alphonse Mucha, and goldsmith Georges Fouquet. A more enigmatic female is flanked by a pair of peacocks in a yellow sapphire, diamond, jade and enamel pendant (2). A silver and enamel brooch depicting an androgynous angel (1), by the Englishwoman Ernestine Mills, is dated 1918, but is very much in the early Arts and Crafts manner.

3

The long-haired, lovely woman in a variety of fin-de-siècle *guises appears in the three jewels on this page. The silver brooch (4) depicts an orchid-bedecked head, the eyes closed in reverie, a six-pointed star marking the brow. The unusual, painted-ceramic brooch (6) is by the Englishman Thomas A. Cook, c. 1910, who was also known for his figural fan designs; the woman on this pin is simply painted and vaguely Oriental in appearance. A stunning angelic head is in the centre of a brooch of 1904 by Parisian Georges Fouquet (5). Second only to Lalique for his goldsmith's work, Fouquet has fashioned here a mystery-laden masterpiece, replete with halo, wings and lotus blossoms, out of gold, enamel, opal, glass, diamonds and pearls.*

4

6

5

BOTANICAL FORMS

1

2

From simple, stylized blossoms to detailed, realistic landscapes, nature in all her forms, real and imaginary, was represented on both Art Nouveau and Arts and Crafts jewellery. René Lalique transformed gold, enamel and glass into a stunning winter-woodland pendant (c. 1899-1900) (2), an icy baroque pearl suspended from the lower branches of its tree frame. Landscape with Trees on the Bank of a Lake, (1) by René Lalique; pencil, pen and ink, and gouache on paper is its preliminary design. The Scotswoman Jessie M. King created this charming silver and enamel pendant (3) for Liberty & Co., c. 1902.

The turquoise matrix, gold and enamel brooch (4) was designed by C.R. Ashbee for the Guild of Handicraft, c. 1899. In fact, it is in the shape of a butterfly, but it can be interpreted as a somewhat floriform design also.

3

4

The long career of Scottish-born Sybil Dunlop began in the early 20th century and lasted until the late 1930s. Out of her studio-shop in Kensington Church Street in London came a plethora of handsome jewels, all hand-fashioned in the Arts and Crafts vein, but the later pieces tinged with Dunlop's unique brand of modernism. This brooch (5), probably of the 1920s, features rich masses of silver, silver-gilt, stones and paste amid the leafy, beaded clusters and coiled tendrils common in early Arts and Crafts goldsmith's work.

5

6

The gold, silver and emerald Tree of Life brooch (6), c. 1905–10, is probably by John Paul Cooper or Edward Spencer, English goldsmiths who worked in a medievalizing manner. The fecund tree is richly detailed, down to the trio of birds amid its leaves. Conversely, the silver, malachite, agate and pearl brooch by Viennese Carl Otto Czeschka (7) is rich in simple, spare stylization. The juxtaposition of the large blossom and the huge stones is jarring, but fin-de-siècle Viennese design did indeed anticipate Art Deco with its bold modernism.

7

TECHNIQUES

The methods of jewellery making employed by the great Art Nouveau goldsmiths were highly sophisticated; their mixture of precious and semiprecious stones and metals was innovative as well, although it soon became commonplace. The maker of the buckle (**1**) was probably French; its workmanship is more primitive than that of the best Gallic jewellery; but the buckle's combination of silver-gilt, seed and baroque pearls and plique-à-jour enamel is typically French (this technique essentially resembles stained glass: its different sections are separated by wires and it has no background). A similar effect to that of plique-à-jour enamel is seen on the lovely gold and opal necklace (**3**) designed by Archibald Knox for Liberty. The opal segments, arranged in a mosaic-like pattern, and the openwork sections in between, make for a novel and sophisticated design, quite different from Knox's applied-enamel pieces.

The totally hand-fashioned brooch (**2**) from the Guild of Handicraft was designed by C.R. Ashbee, its founder, c. 1902–3. Of gold, enamel and turquoise, it features a sailing ship enhanced with lovely applied decoration, from twisted-gold ropes to a fluttering standard.

1

2

3

The silver and amethyst pendant (**4**) was marketed by the London wholesaler Murrle, Bennett & Co., but made in Pforzheim, a major jewellery-manufacturing centre in Germany. Its intertwined scrolls, cruciform shape, applied studs and hammered surface all relate to medieval sources. Though factory made, its hammering would have been done by hand.

Jessie M. King designed this silver and enamel belt buckle (**5**) for Liberty & Co. in 1906. Its two abstract birds are adapted from a design by the Glasgow architect–designer Charles Rennie Mackintosh, but the six stylized blossoms are typical of the many-talented King.

4

5

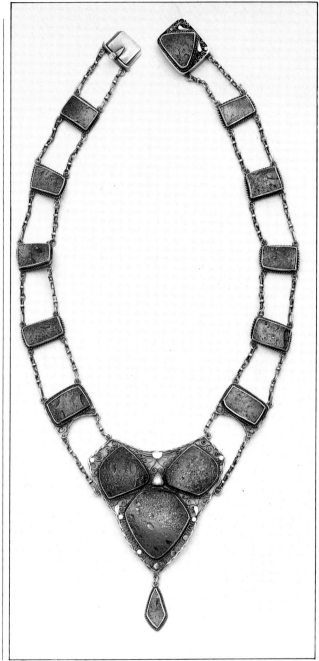

6

The highly unusual necklace (**6**) is of silver set with diamonds and plaques of the type of glass known as "Lava" which was made by Louis Comfort Tiffany. The necklace may have been fashioned by Tiffany, who opened an "art jewellery" department in the family firm, Tiffany & Co., in 1902. Though short-lived (it closed in 1916), it produced some lovely "art jewels" in the Crafts Revival, Byzantine style.

The French joaillier *Cartier created the onyx and paré-set diamond pendant brooch, with its pearl-scattered, detachable tassel. A quintessential moderne jewel, it contains strong Art Deco features: a sense of geometry, a black-and-white colour scheme, a combination of precious and non-precious substances, even a silk-fringe fillip (so much a part of that era's fashion, in both couture and interior design).*

CHAPTER · SEVEN
ART DECO

1920-1939

Following the Bauhaus

·

Innovative materials

·

France at its zenith

PATRICIA BAYER

INTRODUCTION

An intricately fashioned essay in geometry, this 1930s gilded-metal necklace has a strong Machine Age feel. Its stepped sections also relate to Aztec stepped pyramids, an architectural source for some Art Deco jewellery designers. The maker of the necklace is unknown, but the piece is French.

The jewellers of the Art Deco period, which lasted roughly from 1920 to 1939, produced some of the most dazzling pieces ever seen – daring, flamboyant, pristine and even playful. This was the era of the flapper, the Jazz and Machine ages, the between-the-wars (but sandwiching-the-Depression) decades of carefreeness and, concurrently, conservatism, and the artistic output of the period reflected this variety. Unlike the Art Nouveau and Arts and Crafts periods, when noted designers held prime positions and exerted strong influences on other individuals and firms, the Art Deco years were strong on design itself, with many quintessential pieces anonymously designed, unsigned (except for perhaps a retailer's mark), and indeed even of uncertain national origin. So wide-ranging and pervasive a style was Art Deco that similar pieces – necklaces of, say, Bakelite and chrome – were being manufactured in places as disparate as New Jersey and Czechoslovakia.

Materials used by Art Deco jewellery makers ranged from the traditional and precious – diamonds (mostly baguette-cut), rubies, gold, pearls – to the unorthodox and innovative – plastic, chrome, steel. Sturdy, flexible platinum, which was first widely used in the late 19th century, was a relatively new luxury metal that worked well as a setting for emeralds, sapphires and other precious gems, but also complemented such popular semiprecious opaque stones as coral, jade, onyx and lapis lazuli. Costume jewellery, especially with the imprimaturs of the trendsetting couturières Coco Chanel and Elsa Schiaparelli, became ever more popular, outrageous and acceptable – from garish paste chokers and earrings to comical plastic-fish bangles and (from Schiaparelli) a coloured-metal Zodiac-sign necklace.

In the 1920s and 30s, a wide range of jewellery was worn: dangling rhinestone earrings, which showed off the short bobbed haircuts of the Roaring Twenties; bracelets and bangles, the latter often worn en masse on bare upper arms; ultra-long beaded *sautoirs,* which complemented the dropped waistlines of the 1920s; prominent pendants to adorn newly revealed *décolletés* and backs; ubiquitous and multipurpose clips – geometric, floral, figural and usually in pairs – which the 1930's woman attached to her shoes, hat, collar, belt and so on.

The myriad influences contributing to Art Deco jewellery design came from Pharaonic Egypt, the Orient, tribal Africa, Cubism, Futurism, from machines and graphic design, even from buildings, such as stepped Mayan temples and their latter-day descendants, the big-city skyscrapers. Images of animals of speed and grace –the greyhound, the gazelle and the deer – as well as of new-fangled automobiles and aeroplanes were found on both precious and mass-produced jewels. Human subjects were not as common as on Art Nouveau goldsmith's work, but some noted designers depicted them in their works, and,

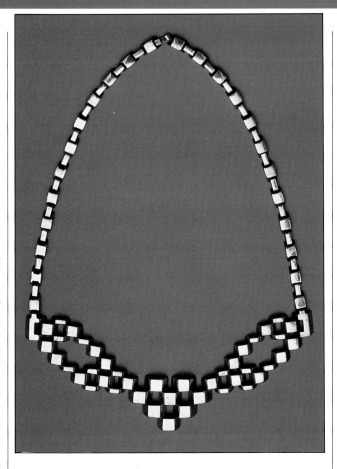

more often, they appeared on inexpensive, anonymous baubles. René Lalique, who created glass jewellery in the 1920s and 30s (having first achieved fame as the premier Art Nouveau goldsmith), moulded some of his pendants with romantic women; stylized African heads formed brooches by Chanel and others; Emile Davide depicted handsome Neo-classical figures, and stylish 1920s women were cut from cheap white metals, sometimes attached by tiny chains to modish canines.

Most of all, however, jewellery of the 1920s and 30s was in thrall to geometry – to circles, arcs, squares, rectangles, triangles and so on, singly and in combination, sometimes pure and unadorned, sometimes slightly embellished to become stylized flowers or leaves or sunbursts, some of pure metal, others of set cabochon stones. Scrolls, ribbons and more elaborate but still relatively uncomplicated forms appear as well, especially in the 1930s. (In the 1940s they would get heavier and chunkier.)

The Art Jewellers of Paris

Paris, of course, was both the source and the trendsetter of Art Deco, which is itself named after the 1925 Exposition des Arts Décoratifs et Industriels Modernes held in Paris. In fact, as early as the 1910s and up to the 1930s it was the fount of innovative fashion; it follows that it should have led the way in *moderne* jewellery.

The Swiss-born designer Jean Dunand (1877–1942), whose hammered-metal and lacquered vases and lacquered furniture and screens were greatly indebted to Asian and other non-Western styles, also designed a small but stunning body of jewellery. Largely of silver lacquered with red and black, Dunand's dangling earrings and earclips, brooches and bracelets, assumed geometric shapes containing equally strong motifs – interwoven or superimposed lines, zigzags, openwork squares and triangles, and so on. Their kinship with the painting of the time is immediately evident, and indeed Dunand often collaborated with Cubist painter and sculptor Jean Lambert-Rucki on his larger projects.

Gérard Sandoz (b. 1902) came from a family of jewellers and began to design starkly geometric pieces for the Sandoz firm while still a teenager. His goldsmith's *oeuvre* dates from a period of just under a decade, yet his output is nonetheless significant within the realm of Art Deco jewellery. The clean lines and delicate craftsmanship of Sandoz's undeniably Machine Age pieces contributed to their significant place in the Art Deco repertoire.

Another gifted goldsmith was Jean Després (1889–1980), whose industrial-design training in the First World War is reflected in his strong pieces. His Machine Age aesthetic may be interpreted as unwieldy and masculine, but it was well suited to the Jazz Age, to the increasingly strong image of the liberated, at times androgynous, woman. In the late 1920s, Després started working with the Surrealist artist Etienne Cournault, whose engraved and painted motifs – one brooch featured a stylized lizard – on mirror-glass added a new design element to Després's earlier, more rigid pieces. Indeed, Després's modernist, industrial-derived pieces (and their contemporary and latter-day imitations) are some of the most desirable for collectors (and wearers) of vintage jewellery today.

Raymond Templier (1891–1968), like Sandoz, came from a family of Parisian jewellers, Maison Templier having been started by his grandfather in the mid–19th century. Templier's designs, like Després's, were boldly geometric, but sported more precious stones, for instance brooches with scatterings of diamonds against stark platinum fields. Templier was especially fond of precious white metals – platinum and silver –and paired them with onyx and other dark stones in stunning pieces (these were regarded as black and white colour combinations, and were wildly popular in the Art Deco period). His designs for the actress Brigitte Helm's jewels in the film *L'Argent*, were marvellously theatrical, especially the blatantly architectonic ear pendants which could be miniature Empire State Buildings or John Storrs sculptures. Templier collaborated

with the designer Michel Percheron and at least once with the Cubist sculptor–painter Gustave Miklos, whose delicate plaster model of an elongated head he translated into a brooch of white and yellow gold.

Paul-Emile Brandt was a Swiss-born jeweller who began working in the Art Nouveau period but evolved into a highly admired Art Deco designer. His cocktail watches, for instance, are richly bejewelled yet strictly geometric. Finally, the Boivin atelier is also worth mentioning here. Opened in 1892 by René Boivin (who later married couturier Paul Poiret's sister, Jeanne), the firm produced

handsome *moderne* designs in the Art Deco period, under the direction of Madame Boivin and her two daughters (René had died in 1917).

The output of these "art jewellers" was small but significant in term of Art Deco design. Much more prolific, and in turn influential, were the mostly long-established jewellery firms producing deluxe pieces – Cartier, Boucheron, Janesich, Chaumet, Mellerio, Fouquet, Vever and Van Cleef & Arpels.

Georges and Jean Fouquet were father and son and both created outstanding Art Deco jewels. Georges (1862–1957), who had also produced Art Nouveau goldsmith's work for La Maison Fouquet (founded by his father, Alphonse), tended toward busier designs, whereas Jean Fouquet (b. 1899), leaned to more geometric forms *à la* Templier's and Sandoz's "art·jewels". The Fouquet firm

Wearable timepieces of all sorts – wristwatches, pendant watches, lapel-brooch watches – were worn by men and women of fashion and means in the Art Deco era. The firm of Louis Cartier, who is credited with the invention of the wristwatch in 1904, fashioned the pendant watch of diamonds, jade, onyx and sapphires; it hangs from a diamond-encrusted bow (both front and back are shown).

also commissioned jewellery from Eric Bagge, the noted architect and interior designer, painter André Leveillé and the premier poster artist–illustrator of the day, A.M. Cassandre.

The Cartier firm, founded in 1847, reached dizzying heights of Art Deco splendour under the direction of Louis Cartier (1875–1942), whose fascination with exotic motifs led to the creation of diamond, ruby and platinum earrings from which hung jade roundels carved with elephants, and a gold and enamel bangle with two carved-coral chimera heads facing each other in the centre. In the 1930s, figural clips and brooches, featuring ornate blackamoor heads, even American Indian squaws and chiefs, were marketed by Cartier and spawned a whole wave of cheap imitations, especially in plastics and base metals. A great deal of carved jade and coral was used on Cartier's rings, brooches, jabot pins, bracelets and necklaces, and motifs such as heavily bejewelled baskets or swags of flowers, berries and leaves (popularly known as "fruit salads" or "tutti frutti") were composed of rich, colourful masses of carved emeralds, rubies, and sapphires amid variously cut and set diamonds. Geometric, or quasi-geometric, arrangements of diamonds, with gemstone highlights, also abounded. Of course, such motifs worked their way into the ever-growing repertoire of costume jewellery, too, with French, American, Czechoslovakian and other factories flooding the market with paste resembling diamonds, rubies, emeralds, even onyx and jade.

The glass jewellery of René Lalique and Gabriel Argy-Rousseau deserves special mention. By the 1920s, the master goldsmith Lalique had become the premier glassmaker of France, and though his main output consisted of vases, tableware and figures, he also created some lovely glass jewellery: pendants, some inspired by open-work Japanese swordguards, or *tsubas,* and moulded with stylized leaf or animal designs, others with insects and lovely female figures, all hanging from silk cords terminating in rich tassels; all-glass rings, moulded with tiny flowers; expandable bracelets of wide rectangular sections decorated with stylized organic designs; necklaces made up partly or wholly of hemispherical, zigzag, floral, foliate or round beads; and brooches on metal backs (often with coloured foil in between) depicting subjects as varied as moths, a satyr, serpents and a grazing stag. *Pâte-de-verre* master Argy-Rousseau also produced jewellery: one diamond-shaped pendant shows a white elephant in a leafy surround; a round medallion features a curtsying ballerina amid a floral border; and another pendant, this one oval, has three scarab beetles, one of many Egyptian motifs made popular in the 1920s following the discovery of Tutankhamun's tomb.

Among the other well-known deluxe jewellers, Mauboussin was noted for his highly colourful pieces, often set in black enamel; Boucheron continued to make

great use of the diamonds which made them famous in the late 19th century, only now they were literally combined with lapis lazuli, jade, coral, onyx and other semiprecious stones; and the jewels of Lacloche Frères, Chaumet, Linzeler & Marshak, Dusausoy and so many other firms sparkled their way into the jewel boxes and on to the necks, arms and clothes of the fashionable rich.

Motifs: from the sublime to the ridiculous

As for precious jewellery in the Art Deco style in other European countries, the little there was was largely derivative, like the Italian G. Ravasco's diamond-studded geometric creations or Theodor Fahrner's later jewels (Fahrner's factory in Pforzheim, Germany, mass-produced Arts and Crafts-style pieces earlier in the century). Some London jewellers, like Asprey and Mappin & Webb, produced Art Deco-style confections, but these are largely unsigned so the designers are unknown. Some British designers however, like Sybil Dunlop, Harold

Stabler and H.G. Murphy, known primarily for their Arts and Crafts-style pieces, produced decidedly *moderne* (though not geometric) jewels.

Georg Jensen's firm in Copenhagen continued to produce silver jewellery in the Art Deco era (and some gold as well), adding sharp geometric forms to its repertoire of stylized motifs. Animal subjects, especially the ever-popular deer, as well as flowers and leaves, adorned brooches, bracelets and buckles, and these in turn were imitated by a host of European and American jewellers.

The indigenous Mexican silver industry was highlighted in the Art Deco era via the talents of an American architect–designer–teacher, William Spratling, who settled in Taxco in 1929. He opened a shop dealing in traditional crafts and also started a school where he trained natives to work with silver and other local substances. Spratling produced some stunning brooches, bracelets and earrings, mostly in silver set with amethysts, but some of gold, all of which had a clean, crisp quality that was highly sympathetic to the

The Parisian jeweller Boucheron created the stunning brooch of jade, diamonds, rock crystal, platinum and gold around 1934. Not only does it make a bold geometric statement with its pavé-set diamond circles and rock crystal half-circles, but its focal point, the carved-jade bird and blossom plaque, gives the brooch a rich Oriental flavour as well.

ART DECO, 1920-1939

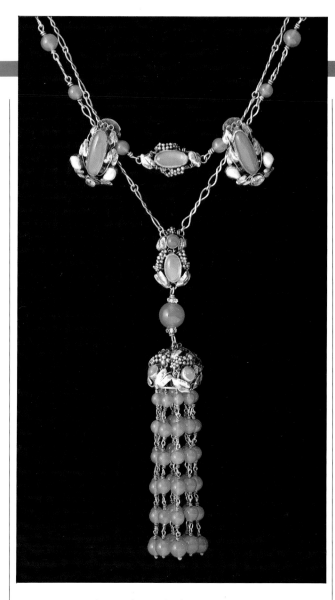

native materials used. A whole community of jewellers sprang up in Taxco around Spratling and his wife.

Many American jewellers and retailers made and marketed precious objects in the high-style French vein. These included Oriental-inspired pieces, like a bracelet from Marsh and Co. (a San Francisco jeweller), its carved-coral plaques alternating with iron sections enclosing Chinese characters; architectonic confections, like a pair of gold Tiffany clips comprising stepped sections of tiny squares, and Egyptian Revival baubles, such as Marcus & Co.'s opal brooch with an elaborate gold setting featuring a Pharaoh and his queen, a scarab beetle and lotus flowers.

Though French designs were often slightly toned down for wealthy, conservative clients, several significant jewellery manufacturers like New York's Oscar Heyman & Brothers, the Bonner Manufacturing Company and Walter P. McTeigue, Inc. provided Saks Fifth Avenue and other exclusive department stores with their creations. Even the

mail-order Sears, Roebuck catalogue featured *moderne* jewellery – diamond wedding rings in handsome geometric settings of platinum, bar pins and pendants with stepped designs, watches with coloured-paste embellishments. Of course, there were American jewellers akin to Cartier (which had a New York branch, as did Van Cleef & Arpels and others). Some of them even had designs made up in Paris for them. In the main, precious American Art Deco *bijoux* tended to be more colourful than their Gallic counterparts.

Geometric rings, clips, brooches, bracelets, lapel watches and necklaces abounded, of precious metals and jewels as well as of base metals or new alloys, paste, marcasite, plastic and stones such as dark red cornelian and apple-green chrysoprase –both chalcedonies, and cheaper to use than coral and jade, which they resembled.

Costume jewellery of the 1920s and 30s – lovely, imaginative, fun, or all three – has surely come into its own in the recent past. In its own time, the fact that Coco Chanel and Elsa Schiaparelli, among other notables, were designing and sporting "fabulous fakes" made them desirable to a wide public. Today, the rage for antique or recent-vintage jewellery has made these 60–70 years old pieces even more popular (though less and less affordable).

The motifs of Art Deco costume jewels range from the sublime to the ridiculous: from stunning geometric configurations of paste to silly plastic cherries dangling from a wooden bar. The former has borrowed its subject from deluxe jewellery of the time, but the latter, a joke, has come about more or less on its own. Animals and people inhabit the world of 1920s and 30s costume jewellery, from gentle silver fawns and playful plastic Scotty dogs to paste, turquoise and marcasite Chinamen and elegant, gilt-metal, cloche-hatted vamps. Flowers in every possible colour, combination and variety sprouted on gilt-metal or silver brooches and pendants, their paste petals glittering shamelessly.

In the late 1930s, sophisticated yet freeform designs began to appear (in both fine and costume jewellery, but especially the latter), with ribbons, bows, loops and scrolls the predominant motifs. The Napier and Coro companies in the USA were at the forefront of the manufacture of these "cocktail jewels", which were highly kinetic and full of energy, unlike the more serene, decorative pieces of a decade or so earlier.

The Scottish-born Londoner Sybil Dunlop, many of whose handcrafted jewels reflect her Arts and Crafts training, created most of her pieces in the Art Deco era. The long 1930s necklace, with tassel pendant and two matching clips, is indeed rife with Arts and Crafts materials and motifs – silver, chrysoprase, moonstone, leafy clusters, coiling wires – but its extreme length, moderne style and beaded tassel are very much of the Jazz Age.

INFLUENCES

The lure of Pharaonic Egypt was strong in the Art Deco era, boosted by the discovery in 1922 of Tutankhamen's tomb. Such motifs as stylized wings and dark, exotic eyes, both seen in an ancient wall-painting (**1**), were eagerly adapted by Art Deco jewellers. In the Egyptian taste is a stunning winged-scarab brooch of 1924 by Cartier (**3**), the body of engraved smoked quartz, the wings of faience and diamonds both dotted with cabochon emeralds. Above that is a similar Cartier design of 1924 for a belt hook (**2**).

1

2

3

4

The outstanding manifestation of Art Deco in the United States was its architecture: soaring, vertical, stepped, sometimes glittering structures began to define Manhattan's evergrowing skyline. Many of these modern temples of industry were masterpieces of both architecture and interior design, like the Chanin Building (Sloan & Robertson, 1929), seen here in an ethereal period drawing (**4**). Some architectonic jewellery was clearly inspired by such skyscrapers; the stepped clips of gold (**5**) are by Tiffany & Co. of New York.

An interesting correlation between industry and goldsmith's work arose in the Art Deco period: some jewellery designers took their inspiration from the structural make-up of factory machines, metallic behemoths like the Colchester Mascot lathe of the 1920s, a detail of which is illustrated (**7**). Parisian Jean Desprès's silver, silver-gilt and onyx bracelet (**8**) of 1930, with its crisp silver cabochons and finely turned "hinges", pays distinct homage to the actual nuts and bolts of the Machine Age. The multihued brooch (**6**), probably French, is of white gold set with six cabochon emeralds. A strange configuration of rubies, diamonds and moonstone completes the design (upside-down, it looks something like an escalator!)

5

6

7

8

PRECIOUS MATERIALS

Precious jewels in the Art Deco period were laden with diamonds, sometimes on their own in blinding masses of icy beauty, sometimes combined with other coloured precious or even semiprecious stones. A pair of Van Cleef & Arpels drop earrings (**1**) feature baguette-cut sapphires and pavé-set diamonds. It was Van Cleef which developed the serti mystérieux, a setting in which stones are placed next to each other with no visible mount.

The gold and diamond necklace (**2**) is probably also by Van Cleef & Arpels.

1

3

4

The pearl, diamond and sapphire brooch–clip (**3**) is by the American firm Marcus & Company, the aquamarine and diamond clips (**4**), which also form a brooch, by an unknown maker. Clips were an important new fashion accessory in the 1930s, mainly due to their versatility.

The stunning "Stalactite" watch and pendant (**5**), 1925, is by Cartier; it is set with diamonds, lapis lazuli, an emerald bead and pearl.

2

5

THE HOUSE OF CARTIER

Founded in Paris in 1847 by Louis-François Cartier, the House of Cartier grew to become one of the world's finest "court jewellers". But it was Louis Cartier (1875-1942), the visionary grandson of the firm's founder, who brought the greatest acclaim to the House of Cartier. His daring, non-traditional designs and his unabashed love of colour and exoticism set him at the forefront of world jewellery design. The year 1910 was a significant one for Cartier: upon viewing the Ballets Russes' production of *Scheherezade*, he and his assistant, Charles Jacqueau, altered not only the firm's palette but also the types of gems they used, opting for semiprecious stones as well as the usual rare gems, sometimes in

Detailed preliminary design for Cartier's "Stalactite" watch

shocking juxtapositions. Coral, black onyx, diamonds and platinum might be combined in one piece, sapphires, emeralds, enamel and gold on another. Motifs both geometric and Oriental appeared on Cartier's jewels, as well as floral and figural designs which were subtly stylized in the taste of the day. Besides decorative *bijoux*, timepieces also comprised a fair portion of Louis Cartier's output, and indeed he is credited with designing the world's first wristwatch as well as what some consider the most significant wristwatch ever made: the Tank® watch. The arts of China, India, Egypt and the Islamic world provided a plethora of subjects for the resourceful Cartier, who then took these motifs and absorbed them into the more rectilinear surroundings of Art Deco.

Below is a colourful trio of precious French joaillerie. The Paris jeweller Boucheron created the elaborate cocktail watch (6); it is a sinuous mixture of diamonds, rubies and platinum. Such ornate timepieces – really bracelets with discreetly hidden watch faces – were highly popular with ladies in the Art Deco period, as were pendant brooches and necklaces with similarly covert timepieces (see the Cartier pendant watch on the previous page). The pendant brooch (7) is made up of diamonds, aquamarines and a giant citrine; its design is subtly geometric, yet without betraying the traditional roots of its maker, the long-established Parisian firm Maison Mellerio. The maker of the arrow-shaped brooch (8), its diamond body set at one end with a giant emerald drop, at the other with a pearl, is not known.

6

7

8

137

STONES

1

2

From the lowly marcasite to the luxuriant baguette-cut diamond – with a rainbow of colourful precious and semiprecious gems (and paste) in between – 1920s and 30s jewellery was rich with stones of every type, cut and hue. The 1930s silver deer pin (1) is set with an array of varisized marcasites, their groupings creating interesting patterns on the animal's body. A 1930s Tiffany & Co. brooch (3), in the unlikely guise of a swordfish, is made up of diamonds, emeralds, sapphires and a ruby. The whirling spiral of brilliant-cut diamonds and calibré-cut sapphires round a cabochon sapphire (2) was made by the New York jeweller Udall & Ballou.

3

4

5

6

The marcasite, chalcedony and silver bracelet (**4**) with a strong geometric design is from the 1930s; such a piece would have been inexpensive and highly popular. Equally popular, but at the upper end of the price range, was the "fruit salad" or "tutti frutti" type jewel created by the finest joailliers out of diamonds mixed with colourful carved rubies, emeralds and sapphires. The diamond and platinum cornucopia brooch (**6**) is overflowing with exquisite carved fruit and leaves; it is French, although its maker is unknown. Another rich mélange of stones, this time of the semiprecious variety, is used in the stunning silver necklace and pendant (**5**), set with a teardrop rock crystal, moonstones, pink coral and pearls. It was hand-crafted by H.G. Murphy in the 1920s; Murphy was apprenticed to the English Arts and Crafts metalsmith Henry Wilson, later setting up his own workshop and teaching at art colleges. Although this pendant still relates to the Arts and Crafts aesthetic that many designers upheld in 20th-century Britain, it is subtly moderne as well: Murphy was fascinated by the exotic forms of the Ballets Russes, and the rich feather-like composition of this ornate pendant could be considered a nod to Diaghilev and company.

A 1940s double-clip brooch in gold, rubies and diamonds.

CHAPTER EIGHT

THE POST-WAR PERIOD

1940-1959

The war legacy

·

The Surrealists

·

Costume jewellery

VIVIENNE BECKER

INTRODUCTION

Jewellery of the 1940s is sometimes called cocktail jewellery, appropriately because it is very much a lively cocktail of 20th-century themes and inspirations. The style evolved from the tail end of Art Deco design, but exuded a robust energy and assertiveness of its own. In the midst of the gloom of World War II, jewellery was bursting with red gold and rubies, ribbons of yellow gold and showers of sapphires, monumental chunks of citrines, aquamarines, amethysts and huge, plump drop-shaped moonstones.

Ingredients of the basic cocktail design were taken from various aspects of Art Deco and the Machine Age. In the 1940s the streamlined, stark architectural lines of modernist jewels were softened into more voluptuous curves, inflated into massive, three-dimensional shapes and coaxed into figurative forms. One of the most striking features of this design is the successful mixture of opposing elements: motifs that are both natural and unnatural, stiff and fluid, static yet full of movement. Early cocktail jewels of the late 1930s or early 1940s still looked geometric and abstract, like bulkier versions of Art Deco pieces; as the decade wore on, they became softer, more full of colour and movement and texture.

Machinery in motion became the most dominant influence on jewels of the 1940s. There was an obsessive interest in tools, machines, how they worked and moved, which manifested itself in jewel design as motifs of screw heads, ball bearings, girders, rods, in metalwork constructed like flexible brickwork or tyre tracks, all reminiscent of the rhythm of the assembly line or a moving staircase.

Cocktail Jewellery

Cocktail jewellery was bred in an atmosphere of enormous change and crisis, of social, economic and political upheaval. Two world wars had brought a drastic redistribution of wealth, and women had now won a good measure of independence and authority. The new breed of working women created a market for fashionable ready-to-wear clothes and accessories, while financial difficulties also forced some wealthy customers to make economies without sacrificing style or outward confidence. However grim their everyday lives, most women went to the cinema and were exposed, first-hand, to all the glamour of Hollywood. Glamour and escapism was much in demand in the 1940s, yet there was simply not the same amount of money to spend on masses of diamonds and platinum. Instead, to achieve the effect of massive magnificence, limited quantities of gold were eked out and cleverly wrought to look like heavy chunks of sumptuous metal. Gold was often stamped out from thin sheets to give the effect of substantial weight.

As sleek geometry gave way to sculptural forms, there was a move towards the use of wide expanses of sweeping metal, rose pink gold or rich yellow-gold, wrought into gauche swirls, whorls, drapes. In contrast to the chic black and white of the mid-1920s, colour became all-important, integrated by the use of coloured gold and transparent semi-precious stones. Metal was textured for added interest: a pattern of perforated hexagons, creating a honeycomb design, was a favourite feature of Van Cleef & Arpels in the 1940s, or little overlapping semi-circles like shiny scales. Gold mesh, imitating gauze or lattice and basketwork, became especially popular in the late 1940s and 1950s. Fabric motifs predominated and gold looked like drapes, bows, knots, with added bouncy movement of tassels or bobbles.

In contrast to the static geometry of Art Deco, movement became the central feature of cocktail jewellery design. There was a contrived stiffness to the pleats and folds and drapes of cocktail jewels, but the overall effect was one of wild movement and flexibility. Chain was often ribbed or folded like a concertina in a style known as gas pipe for obvious reasons, or it could be knitted into a tight mesh

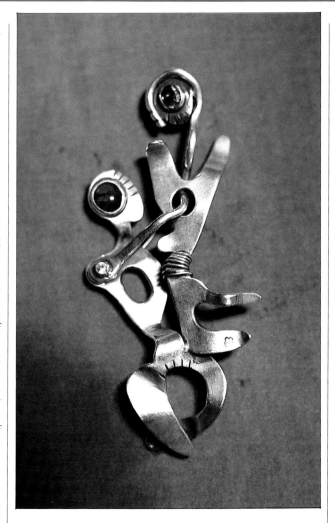

148

rope of herringbone pattern, or bouncy spring like coils.

The air of unreality that touched the 1920s and 30s still affected the ever-popular flower jewels of the 1940s and 50s. Gold and gem-set blossoms were made like naive, shiny buttercups or stiff, star-shaped flowers. Van Cleef & Arpels produced the most spectacular flowers of the period, using their new invisible settings, in which masses of tiny, square-cut rubies or sapphires were held from behind by a gold framework only, so that no means of setting could be seen from the front.

Amusing, figurative motifs, and cartoon-like animals gradually crept into jewel design in the mid-1940s. There were stiff childlike figures of scarecrows, clowns, gardeners or flower-sellers and, most characteristic of all, the ballerina, set with tiny coloured gems. The range of amusing figures and animals was one aspect that continued into the 1950s. It was Cartier, and particularly the designer Jeanne Toussaint, who helped build up the fashion for fantasy creatures, for perky animal and bird of paradise jewels. The big cats, the panthers and leopards, which have become the luxurious but poignant symbols of the Duchess of Windsor, were perfected in Cartier's workshops in the 1940s and 50s.

The Second World War in Europe had depleted the jewellery-making industry. Jewellers' premises had been destroyed and many of its skilled workforce had left to join the army or were co-opted into war work, as jewellers were well equipped to undertake precision engineering. Cartier's craftsmen, for example, spent the war making camera parts and navigational equipment. Jewellers who did manage to continue in business found precious metals and stones scarce – sometimes even unobtainable. However, with the liberation of Paris in October 1944, the great names – Boucheron, Cartier, Chaumet and Van Cleef & Arpels – were able to open for business again.

The boldness of 1940s jewellery belonged to the major grand-jewels houses, the leaders in the field. Van Cleef & Arpels, Boucheron, Chaumet, Lacloche, Mauboussin, Mellerio and their neighbours in and around the Place Vendôme all excelled in the cocktail style. As the influence of war was less pervasive in the United States, American jewellers or New York branches of Parisian houses flourished at this time, in particular, Paul Flato, John Rubel, Verdura, Traebert and Hoeffer. In Italy, Bulgari led a band of jewellers working in the cocktail mood, and in Switzerland major watch firms produced stylish cocktail wristwatches, popular accessories of the period. In England, trade was slowly resumed after the war and the prevailing style in Europe was adopted gradually by London manufacturers such as D. Shackman and Byworth.

Newly liberated from the deprivation of war-time, the designers of costume jewellery felt free to experiment, making pieces out of gold-plated base metals, silver gilt

and paste which were hard to distinguish from those worth one hundred times as much. Costume jewellery design even began to influence those who worked in traditional precious metals and stones.

The Fashionable Fifties

As with most ages, during the 1950s, there was a two-tier system of jewellery: expensive gem-set pieces, made by famous jewellery houses, in mainstream fashions; or the artist-craftsman's jewellery, made in smaller workshops from less expensive materials, in which design and artistic spirit were the most important elements.

In expensive jewellery, a sophisticated all-white, all diamond look predominated. The emphasis in design was on movement, and to achieve this soignée effect, diamonds of different cuts and shapes were used together to create, swirls, twirls, fans, waterfalls and cascades. The little rod-shaped baguette diamond, beloved of the Art Deco jewellers, was enormously popular once again, but was now incorporated into far more voluptuous, curvaceous patterns. Huge majestic flower sprays were also

This gold brooch and earring set combines two distinct styles: the chunkiness of 40s cocktail jewellery in the ribbon-like curls of the leaves, with the much lighter and more delicate spray-forms that could be found dotting many a lapel in the 1950s. The transition from the lightly contained designs of the 30s, through the beginnings of movement in the cocktail jewellery of the 40s to the light swirls and open forms in the 50s, reflected a decisive change of mood amongst designers — a mood caught from society in general who were wanting new and "modern" designs.

INTRODUCTION

typical of the late 1940s and 50s, politely luscious, extravagant blooms, their petals pavé set with diamonds or coloured gems, mixed often with butter-yellow gold which was increasingly popular from the late 1930s through the 1940s and 50s. A combination of gold filigree wire or lattice openwork with diamonds was popular around 1950, concocted into stylized flower sprays with the dynamic movement of the 1940s and the icy sophistication of the 1950s.

Alongside the traditional, majestic white diamond look,

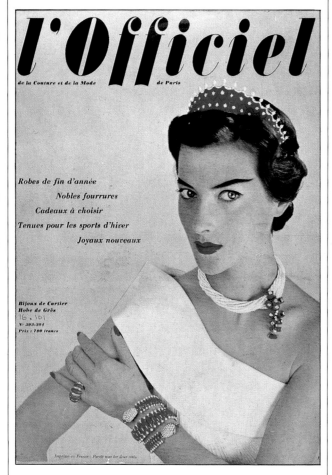

Despite the occupation of France during World War II, the Paris firm of Cartier still maintained its dominant position in the world of luxury jewellery, as shown by this glamorous cover picture from L'Officiel from 1951. The name of Cartier is still synonymous with luxury and opulence although the market for their jewels must have changed considerably. Many of the noble houses who traditionally patronized the major jewellery firms, no longer have the power, wealth, or even perhaps the desire, to commission sumptuous jewels. Much of the market is now in the Middle East, where the traditions for the display of rich decoration and splendid body adornment remain.

expensive jewellery in the 1950s featured coral and turquoise, mixed with flounces of bristling yellow gold and scatterings of diamonds. Some abstract designs heralded the new organic mood of the 1960s, others were based on cocktail age flowers, birds insects. The coral ladybird, alone or poised on a gold flower or leaf, its body set with tiny diamonds, enriched with enamels perhaps, onyx or lapis lazuli, was a hallmark of 1950s jewellery design and a favourite motif at Cartier. Starfish jewels were worn in the 1950s, in gold and diamonds or perhaps with smooth coral tentacles, while shells and seahorses illustrated the mystery

and magic of the ocean. Birds and animals in many cases also became more fantastic, the static quality of 1940s designs giving way to extra vitality and a sense of soaring movement, particularly in the design of sweeping tail feathers, wings stretched backwards against the wind, and quirky inquisitive heads pointed towards the light. Pierre Sterlé in Paris was the champion of this style of the 1950s. He used an almost baroque combination of coloured gems, precious and semi-precious, mixing amethysts with turquoises for example, and generously adding fringes of gold mesh or chain, gold textured wings or feathers, enlivened with showers of diamonds.

Fine Art

A number of prominent painters and sculptors moved into jewellery-making as a new area of artistic expression. The first of these were the Swiss sculptor Alberto Giacometti and the American sculptor, best known for his mobiles, Alexander Calder. Ernst, Cocteau, de Chirico, Man Ray, Tanguy and Dubuffet followed, each of whom produced small collections.

By the early 1960s, Georges Braque had designed more than 130 pieces which were exhibited in the Musée des Arts Décoratifs in Paris. These featured Braque's unique interpretation of mythological scenes, and were often made in textured gold superimposed on slabs of cut stone, rhodocrosite or lapis lazuli.

Even more prolific was the Spanish surrealist, Salvador Dali. He produced a large collection of surreal pieces – soft watches, a cross of gold sugar lumps, an enamelled platinum eye with a jewelled tear dripping, a golden heart containing a sack of pulsating rubies, an elephant with spider's legs. Many of these pieces were unwearable, but Dali claimed his work was in the tradition of Benvenuto Cellini, Sandro Botticelli and Leonardi da Vinci. He also claimed that his work encompassed "physics, mathematics, architecture, nuclear science, the pyscho-nuclear, the mystico-nuclear" and that it was "a protest against emphasis on the cost of the materials of jewellery". In these aims, he was anticipating much of the contemporary approach.

In Italy, other fine artists began to get involved in jewellery. The first was the sculptor Bruno Martinazzi. Many of his pieces are strongly sculptural, with an emphasis on texture. He builds his designs layer by layer, often incorporating different coloured golds and even platinum in a single piece. Gemstones – usually diamonds – are pavé-set as highlights. He was followed by the Pomodoro brothers – Arnaldo, a sculptor and architect, and Gio, a painter and graphic designer – whose work has a more deliberate, planned quality, almost as if incorporating other disciplines into their jewellery work.

In Germany, aeronautical engineer Friedrick Becker turned professional goldsmith in 1947 and brought with him an aesthetic built on machine engineering and aerospace technology. His pieces are composed of polished, geometric forms, sometimes even with moving parts.

Democratic Designs

As far as less expensive jewellery was concerned in the 1950s, there was an exciting move towards 'modern' artistic silver jewels, very much in tune with the general rather austere style of the decorative arts. Silver suited the smooth, floating lines characteristic of Fifties designs in general. Its subtle tones and textures were perfect for capturing organic designs, the spindly Calder-inspired spirals, but at the same time they were strong enough to interpret the sharp, zigzag motifs of the oncoming electronic age –the "electrocardiogram" element of Fifties design.

From the 1930s, Scandinavian jewellers often used the simple shapes they derived from folk art to produce new "democratic" designs. These deliberately avoided the over-ornamentation which other European jewellers used to impress their noble clientele. The smooth, clean lines and reverence for natural materials which typified the Scandinavian approach found itself in the ascendancy in a postwar period where the grip of social class had been eroded. As the style was refined it became a growing influence on other European designers.

The early exponent of the Scandinavian style was Georg Jensen. Trained as a sculptor, he specialized in a distinctive, sculptural style, almost always figurative or organic, but highly stylized and precise. Jensen died in 1935, but his Copenhagen-based company became a major influence after the war. The firm's enlightened artistic policy was maintained by Jensen's son, Soren Georg Jensen. Hanna Ditzel, the architectural designer, has worked for Jensen since 1954, and a host of other famous names designed for the firm – Herlow, Koppel, Malinowski, Mohl-Hansen, Pedersen and Rohde. Henning Koppel's designs for Jensen are amongst the most distinctive of the age.

In America, the industry was less affected by the war, and started off the postwar period with an exhibition in 1946 in New York's Museum of Modern Art where some 135 pieces were exhibited by 46 artists. Two years later, twice as many artists exhibited at Minneapolis's Walker Art Center, and by 1955 a Museum of Contemporary Crafts was founded in New York. In 1960, the US Government established the American Crafts Council, which opened regional centres throughout the country where craftsmen could hold seminars, workshops and exhibitions.

But America did not just have the seed corn of its own native talent to depend on. It was awash with hundreds of European artists and jewellers, forced out of Europe by the war and bringing with them the influence of Bauhaus. In 1940, Margaret de Patta began studying under Lazlo Moholy-Nagy, first at a summer school, then at the School

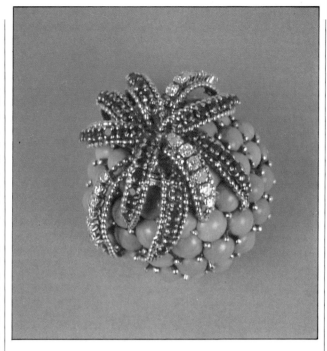

The established companies who still produce luxury goods have seen no need to experiment with new design concepts. Much of their work relies on classic jewellery forms, exquisitely fabricated and set with flawless gems, like this piece from Van Cleef & Arpels (late 1950s-60s). It is set with rubies, turquoises and diamonds—with organic imagery in evidence, but there is no attempt at realism. This jewellery is for a world of glamour, set apart from the harsh realities of life.

of Design in Chicago he had set up. Influenced by Picasso, she created miniature silver sculptures, and became a seminal figure in American jewellery with her bold use of new materials and techniques.

The Bauhaus ideology of breaking with all traditional restraints found fertile soil in the USA. Sam Kramer began incorporating *objets trouvés* (found objects) in his jewellery, aping other contemporary American fine artists who were using the sculptural and painterly technique of assemblage. These works further eroded the barriers between jewellery and sculpture. He even anticipated the 1960s by drawing inspiration from science fiction comics.

Kramer's shop in New York's Greenwich Village encouraged others. Harlem-born black artist Arthur Smith moved to Greenwich Village in the 1940s and began to produce large neckpieces and bracelets intended to be body adornments rather than simple fashion accessories. These too anticipated the revolution in jewellery that was to come about in the 1960s.

INFLUENCES

1

2

Paris resumed the lead in couture fashion after the Second World War. Styles retained their simplicity, but indicated a move away from frugality with longer skirts and more attention to detail. These tweed suits from Balmain (*1*), illustrated in Picture Post in 1953, show feminine nipped-in waists and more complex pattern-cutting than would have been considered sensible in the war years. Jewellery was worn as another mere detail. Small, pretty brooch and earring sets were popular for everyday wear, like the gold and citrine set in the bottom of the picture (*2*). Flowers were an endless source of design inspiration during the 1950s.

4

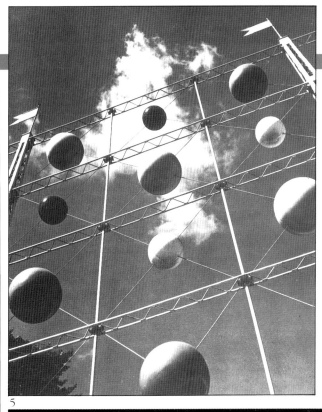

5

Scientific developments astounded and fascinated everybody. Designers began to use scientific iconography with striking effect. Edward Mills designed this screen (**5**) for the Festival of Britain held on London's South Bank in 1951. Magnified molecular structures were also the source of inspiration for textile and furniture designers.

The gold and diamond brooch (**6**) that miniaturizes the path of the planets around the sun celebrates science and natural phenomena while remaining an intriguing, attractive and lightweight design.

Developments in fine art had their equivalent in the more progressive jewellery. Sculptural concerns of mass, form and expressive abstraction, as seen in the bronze Reclining Figure by Henry Moore (**3**) made in 1953–4 could be seen on a smaller scale with jewellery intended as an art form and not just a fashion accessory. This was evident particularly in the work of the Danish firm of Georg Jensen. This ring (**4**) from the 1950s owes more to sculpture than to jewellery traditions.

3

6

TRADITIONAL LUXURY

Colourful and exotic images caught the imagination of Europeans still experiencing the austerity of the war years. These three brooches (**1**) from Sterlé of Paris in the 1940s capture the natural sweeping asymmetry of flora and fauna, something not seen in the more constrained Art Deco designs. They seem to symbolize freedom and romanticism, transporting the imagination to tropical gardens of a mysterious underwater world.

Despite its passage into public ownership in the 1960s the firm of Cartier still dominates the world of luxury jewellery. The famous series of leopard and panther jewellery remains as sought after today as ever, as the sale of this sapphire and diamond panther clip (**3**) from the Duchess of Windsor's collection testifies. Made by Cartier in 1949, the panther is pavé-set with diamonds and calibre-cut sapphire spots with pear-shaped yellow diamond eyes. It is crouching on a large cabochon sapphire.

The older firms famous for their exquisite gem-set jewellery tend to stay with more traditional designs. Another family firm from Paris, Boucheron, produced this fan-shaped brooch (**4**) in the 1950s. With its Oriental prettiness it could easily have adorned a genteel Victorian lady, showing nothing in its design that would place it in the 20th century.

Jewellers returned to more literal translations of flowers, birds and animals in the 1940s and 50s. The mushroom brooch (**2**) possibly by Van Cleef & Arpels appears charmingly naïve. The stalks illustrate a trend towards the use of wire as a means of creating surface texture and lightening the weight of jewellery, both visually and physically.

1

2

3

The restrictions of 1937 did not prevent Van Cleef & Arpels from producing this sumptuous Jarretière bracelet (**6**). To aid the reflective quality of the gems the cushion-shaped sapphires and baguette diamonds are invisibly set – a technique invented by the maker. The ring is by the American "King of Diamonds", Harry Winston. He bought the diamond in the collection of Washington hostess Evalyn Walsh McClean in 1940 and sold it the following year to the Duke and Duchess of Windsor.

6

5

The Paris family firm of Chaumet specialized in tiaras and jewelled liveries for Indian potentates. Like other famous companies they cultivated the custom of royal families around the world, which may explain the mother-of-pearl globe in their brooch "Le Spectacle du Monde" (**5**), of the late 1950s-60s, but not its surrealistic setting in a jester's hat.

The styles of the younger jewellers who started out at the end of the 1950s can be easily distinguished. Since 1954, De Beers have organized the annual Diamonds International awards, which both encouraged new jewellers to be innovative and gave them publicity. The rings (**7**) are four British winners from the early 1960s: left, John Donald; centre top, Geoffrey Turk; centre bottom, Podolsky; right, David Thomas.

7

EVERYDAY ACCESSORIES

The smart tailored suits worn by women in the 1950s provided an excellent background for brightly coloured, cheerful jewellery. Neat brooches, often worn on the lapel of a coat or jacket, were popular everyday wear. The enamelled silver basket of flowers from the 1950s (**1**) is a timeless and nostalgic reminder of the pastoral idyll close to the heart of many a city worker. Many more women were earning a wage by this time and able to buy good quality costume jewellery.

1

2

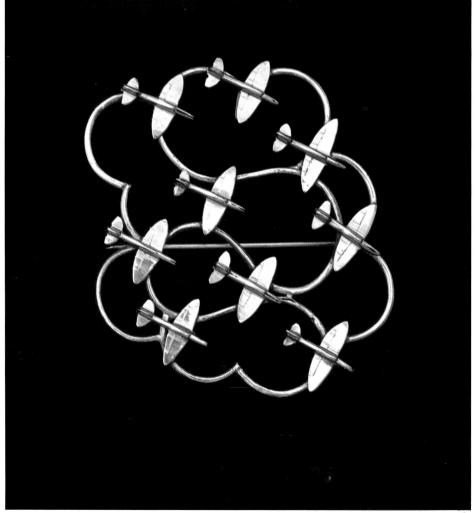

3

Gently swaying floral sprays again lent colour and an interesting curvaceous form to brooches in the 1950s. This example in silver gilt and chrysoprase (**2**) is typical of the period. The emotive use of bunches of flowers created a feeling of joie de vivre and romanticism, very aptly coinciding with the end of rationing and utility product designs.

Wartime images were still fresh in everybody's memory. A formation of little silver aeroplanes sweeping across a female chest shows a fair degree of humour (**3**), but no doubt it also held deeper significance for the wearer. It was quite common for military insignia and miniature hardware, like boats and planes, to appear in jewellery during the war.

By the 1940s and 50s costume jewellery was rivalling the real thing. Improved technology in casting, plating and creating paste gems made better quality "fakes" a feasible alternative to gold and gemstones (see **5**). The glamour of the Hollywood movie stars and wealthy socialites could now be emulated by the middle class woman, helped by good ready-to-wear copies of couture clothing and skilfully produced costume jewellery.

Many more people had the money and time to entertain, as well as the chance to look spectacular at an affordable price, and so the era of the cocktail party (originally just a pursuit of the wealthy), took off. Cocktail jewellery was very popular, and its chunkiness lent itself to costume copies. Art Deco imagery was still evident, but more fun and movement came in with bows and swirls and folds (**4**). The popularity of costume jewellery made the market dynamic and competitive. Designers could be freer and less conservative, and in many ways left the traditional jewellers lagging behind.

5

4

6

Witty images like the marcasite French poodle brooch (**6**) were used to make the business-like tailored suit more fun. Animals shaped like Walt Disney cartoon characters and resplendent Birds of Paradise signified the wish for a brighter and less troubled future.

ABSTRACT INNOVATORS

The northern European move away from the glitz of burnished gold and diamonds can be seen in this white gold and lapis lazuli bracelet (1) from Amsterdam in the 1950s. The surface decoration is provided by the slight change in height and angle of the segments. With its machine-like finish the appeal is in the piece's subtle simplicity and precision.

1

2

MARGARET DE PATTA (1903-64)

The term "artist/jeweller" came into its own in the 1970s, but those who pioneered the concept can be picked out from much earlier. Margaret de Patta was one of them. She studied painting and sculpture at the Academy of Fine Arts in San Diego (1921-23), the California School of Fine Arts in San Francisco (1923-25) and the Art Students League in New York (1926-29). Without losing her artistic intentions, she turned her attention to jewellery in 1929. To be free from craft traditions and technical limitations she studied and mastered many jewellery skills.

A summer school in 1940, run by the ex-Bauhaus artist Lazlo Moholy-Nagy, had a significant effect on her development.

De Patta's 1947 silver and quartz crystal brooch reflects her interest in expressive artforms, which grew from her early training as a painter and sculptor.

Bauhaus ideas reinforced the validity of her experimental methods: counter to the traditions of the time she used such materials as stainless steel and plastic in her work, and in 1941 she collaborated with the lapidary Francis J. Sperisen, exploring the reflective qualities of stones with new cuts. Her work was so well received that in 1946 she began to produce prototypes for manufacture. Her jewellery proved to be a successful competitor to costume jewellery, but she never lost sight of her original aim to create expressive artforms with her jewellery.

Margaret de Patta was generous in her encouragement to other jewellers, teaching and lecturing until her death, and was active in the promotion and development of jewellery via the Metal Arts Guild, Designer Craftsmen in California and the American Crafts Council.

"Individuality", the watchword of the 1970s, has never been totally absent from jewellery. This necklace (2) is by Sah Oved, second daughter of a country doctor, and born in 1900 as Gwendolen Ethel Rendle. She found a rich source of inspiration for her work when she met Mosheh Oved. He was a Polish Jew whose culture and folklore strongly influenced Sah's work. Cameo Corner, his shop in London's Museum Street, provided a treasure chest of raw materials for her highly original pieces. She decided early in her life to be a jeweller, but worked with little formal training. Finally she studied silversmithing at the Central School of Arts and Crafts, London, during the 1950s.

3

Artists have often turned their hand to jewellery design. Jean Arp (born 1888 in France) produced this rather surreal silver and pebble brooch in the 1950s (**4**). Salvador Dali's imagery also translated particularly well into extravagant jewellery and George Braque designed an impressive range in his later years.

4

Modernism affected designers all over Europe, but Scandinavia led the field with their profound modernist jewellery designs after the war. The firm of Georg Jensen in Denmark influenced many other jewellers with their progressive artistic policy. Their many different designers, were each credited by name for the individual pieces they contributed to Jensen's. The starkly simple gold pendant from the late 1950s or early 1960s) (**3**) is by Bent Gabrielson Pederson, and is typical of the Scandinavian style. The shift from decorative work blurred the dividing line between sculpture and jewellery. In the 1950s, the Pomodoro Brothers in Italy began working and exhibiting as both sculptors and jewellers (**5**). Arnaldo (born 1926) studied architecture, sculpture and stage design, Giorgio (born 1930) studied painting, graphic art and sculpture.

5

159

ABSTRACT INNOVATORS

Until the Second World War everyone looked to France for the latest trends, from fashion to fine art. From the 1940s, America began to dominate the world with modern art and popular culture. Neither American styling, the cool, refined Scandinavian jewellery or the sculpturally formed work from Germany and Italy had many parallels in France. The concise elegance of this French gold torque from the 1950s (**1**) is atypical of the national trend. The rough surface texture of the cast rectangles and the spare curve of wire owe their origins to Scandinavia, but the overall delicacy produced by the softness of the chain give it a French flavour.

1

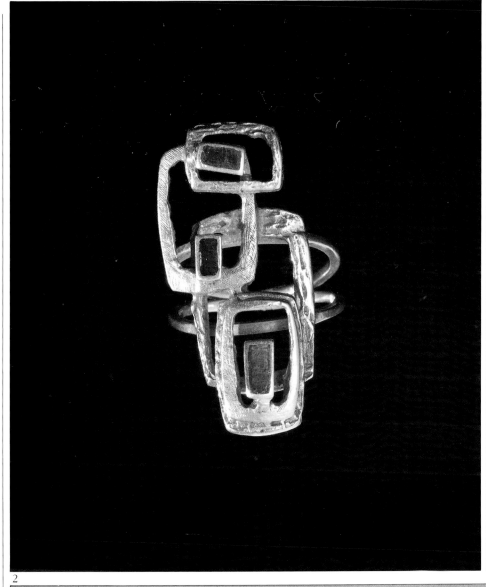

2

Abstraction in painting was the most significant development this century. The distillation of the visual imagery filtered down to every design discipline. This gold and enamel ring (*2*) from the 1950s epitomizes the stylistic use of rough rectangular forms, cast metal with roughly textured surface finishes and powerful colours used sparingly for maximum effect. The gold, diamond and emerald bracelet (*3*) by John Donald (born 1938), shows how the new breed of college-trained jewellers embraced modernism and experimentation with individual flair in the late 1950s and 60s. Donald was one of the first to use natural crystals in his work.

3

William Harper's "Temptation of St Anthony", in gold cloisonné enamel on silver, gold,
aluminium, opal, tourmaline, mirror, freshwater pearl, ivory and bone.

CHAPTER NINE

CONTEMPORARY JEWELLERS

1960-1989

Abstraction

·

Modern materials

·

Jewellery as art

·

Imagery from space and technology

HELEN CRAVEN

INTRODUCTION

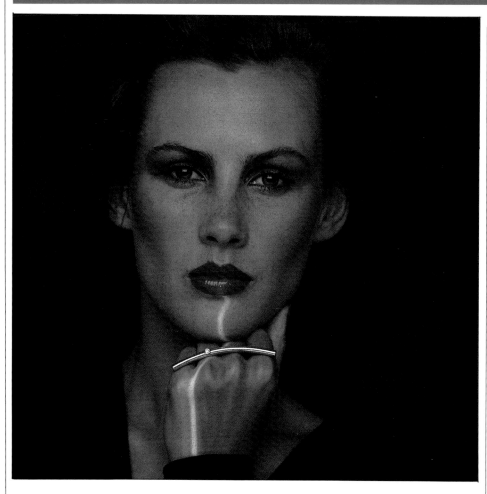

The stark simplicity of minimalism achieves a different perspective when applied to jewellery. Friedrich Becker uses simple forms, as in this gold and diamond ring, but his concern is to make his pieces come to life with the natural movements of the wearer. The curves of the body and the curves created by movement transform his technical forms into inspired expressiveness.

In the last 30 years, the Western world has experienced unprecedented technological advances, with immense social changes following in their wake. Although jewellery – as a decorative art – has never been in the vanguard of cultural change, many contemporary jewellers have reflected changing social mores by using their ingenuity and expertise to explore the medium and even question its values.

Continuing Traditions

Not all has been change, though. The most famous names in the jewellery world – Cartier, Bulgari, Boucheron, Asprey and Tiffany – have remained faithful to their exclusive and wealthy clientele and continue to produce jewellery in the traditional "grand manner". The established companies still devise sumptuous designs in precious metals and exquisite gemstones as status symbols, heirlooms and investments. In recent years many consumers of this grand jewellery have been from the Middle East, where tradition still demands the formal display of wealth and rank.

In England, the 1960s brought a new generation of artist-jewellers, as well as a new wealthy self-made clientele. There was a great demand for a different species of jewellery: less formal, more modern and an expression of the affluent decade.

In 1961 the Worshipful Company of Goldsmiths held an influential milestone exhibition of modern jewellery which revealed the potential of jewellery as a medium for artistic self-expression. 1960s British jewellery, epitomized by the work of Andrew Grima, was self-consciously modern, aiming to break with the past. Grima, for example, came to jewellery making from engineering. In 1946, he began producing traditional jewellery for his own H.J. company, although by 1961 he was taking a much freer approach. Many of his works were based on *objets trouvés*. He managed to capture the texture of leaves, twigs and bark in precious metal, casting his pieces in 18-carat gold and studding them with gemstones.

Alongside Grima, jewellers like John Donald, Louis Osman, Gillian Packard and David Thomas also developed contemporary designs using new images celebrating scientific achievement, for example molecular and cell structures. Materials were chosen more for their aesthetic value than for their monetary worth. Natural organic shapes were incorporated in the designs; uncut crystals and minerals were often used.

Gradually semiprecious stones took over from crystals: tiger's eye, coral, lapis lazuli, and black onyx. Non-precious stones were popular and when precious stones were used they were an integral part of an overall design, not clustered together for their own sake.

In New York Jean Schlumberger reigned supreme over Tiffany in the 1960s, and he too was responsible for shifting the emphasis away from valuable stones and towards "artistic" content in design. Schlumberger had progressed from making costume jewels for Schiaparelli in Paris in the 1930s to making real, exotic, fantasy jewels in New York in the 1940s and 50s. In 1956 Walter Hoving invited Schlumberger to set up his own department in Tiffany, and to become vice-president of the store. Schlumberger embarked on a series of fantastic, rich and sumptuous jewels, tinged with baroque splendour, created through the 50s, 60s and 70s. Schlumberger's subject matter was almost always organic, sometimes heraldic, always luscious and startling, reflecting the curiosities and marvels of nature. He loved colour and dared to mix sapphires and emeralds, amethysts and aquamarines, spinels, turquoises, with generous lashings of yellow gold and brilliant enamels.

In the 1960s the artistic approach was taken much further. Theories of the Bauhaus continued to influence many art education institutions and designers throughout Europe. They encouraged the search for a universal, rational, simple beauty – a "democracy" of form. This influence can been seen throughout Europe well into the 1970s, particularly in Holland and Britain, and although there have been many other theories and methods of teaching design since, the rigours of the Bauhaus teaching with its desire to define forms in a minimal way are still held as fundamentals by many designers.

Jewellery as Art

The art world in the 1940s and 50s was dominated by the American Abstract Expressionists. Artists saw themselves as pioneers, liberating the world from the bonds of tradition. These ideas pervaded the whole world of art and design, and found expression in what were called Studio Crafts which usually demanded that a single individual was responsible for both designing and making unique hand-crafted pieces. In the USA itself, Australia, the UK and many other countries, the teaching of Studio Crafts became a part of the art school curriculum, and jewellery making found a new role as an expressive art form.

Meanwhile, in Germany and France, the apprenticeship system remained strong, and the skill of the jeweller was respected as such. German colleges still teach rigorous technical courses as well as fine art, and many teachers are noted jewellers in their own right: Herman Jünger at the Munich Academie der bildenden künste, Friedrich Becker in Düsseldorf and Reinhold Reiling in Pforzheim, for example. Reiling trained as an engraver as well as a goldsmith and his early pieces were geometric and strongly influenced by Scandinavian designers. By the late 1960s, his work had become free and asymmetric. He studded his pieces with cabochon and facet-cut stones and began introducing texture. There is also a freedom from traditional restraint that characterizes American work and the influence of the North and South American Indians is detectable. Their bold expressiveness can be seen in the work of many jewellers, such as Robert Ebendorf, William Harper, Mary Lee Hu, Richard Mawdsley, Stanley Lechtzin, Earl Pardon and many more. Many of America's leading jewellers are also teachers passing on their experience and enthusiasm to new generations of artist–jewellers.

With the breaking down of traditional barriers between different art disciplines, an increasing number of jewellers have presented their work as art. In England, David Watkins of the Royal College of Art in London first trained as a sculptor and then turned to jewellery. His neckpieces and bracelets have always appeared like sculptures that fit on and relate to the human body, rather than as anything purely decorative. His work has usually been exhibited in galleries with an artist's eye and attitude guiding its considered presentation. Dr Kevin Coates is very much an artist who has chosen to express his ideas and themes through sculptural jewellery design, using precious and semiprecious materials. Both spiritual and intellectual, the brilliant jewels or miniature sculptures each tell a story, perpetuate a timeless myth, or bring a creature to life. David Courts and Bill Hackett work mainly to commission in precious materials. Their designs' are characterized by a sleek sensuality, their themes taken from unusual, often macabre, aspects of nature: a frog's skeleton, for example, or a crayfish.

This growing more towards "artistic" could be seen developing among several other jewellers in the early 1970s. Certain German jewellers, noted for their technical excellence and attention to detail, also presented their designs as "pictures". Ulrike Bahrs and Norbert Muerrle produced figurative, pictorial pieces in forms that served either as jewellery or as graphic images. Gerd Rothman presented stickpins in a frame with a painted background. Gijs Bakker and Robert Smit from Holland and Claus Bury from Germany showed an affinity with Conceptual Art in

being concerned as much with showing their ideas as with exhibiting a finished product. Helga Zahn from the UK showed Art Language to be her influence, with a 1975 brooch which included the words: "The philosophers have only interpreted the world in various ways, the point however is to change it. Marx."

New Concepts, New Materials, New Techniques

Inevitably, when jewellers were placed alongside fine artists and other designers, they were caught up in the desire of the younger generation for a voice and identity of its own. In the boom years of the 1960s, reflecting the sexual revolution that was taking place in the West, there

Many jewellers in the last twenty years have experimented with combinations of different metals for contrasts in colour, texture and form. Traditionalists have frowned on combining precious and base metals, but the ends often justify the means, as can be seen with this brooch by Barbara Christie made of silver and nickel.

INTRODUCTION

were significant changes in the fashions designed and worn by young people. Younger designers responded also to the social changes that were spreading across Europe.

In the UK, a "non-conformist" jeweller who stands out at this time is Gerda Flockinger. In 1961, when she was appointed to run the new jewellery course at Hornsey College of Art, she developed a programme that not only taught traditional skills, but also encouraged experimentation. Her own work exhibited an irreverence to the traditional treatment of precious metals. She melted the surfaces of her jewellery to exploit the natural texture that was created by a combination of skill and accident. She fused wire and shapes cut from sheet metal, setting semi-precious stones and pearls into the finished form so that they appeared like intriguing decorative blisters, bubbling from the surface. The overall impression is of an organic form that has grown miraculously rather than of a fabricated artefact.

Patricia Tormey went even further, slamming molten gold between layers of textured charcoal or dropping it into a tray of lentils. Her best-known pieces, though, are minute, often erotic, tableaux cast in gold.

In Holland, traditionally trained jewellers Gijs Bakker and Emmy van Leersum turned the very notion of jewellery on its head when they experimented with the simple forms that became both clothing and jewellery. They also made large neckpieces that imposed physical constraints on the wearer. Their questioning of the nature of jewellery affected many other jewellers in Europe, particularly in the UK and their native Holland. When did jewellery become clothing? When did it become unwearable? When did it become sculpture? These questions continued to be asked for the next 15 to 20 years.

Some contemporary jewellers have shown an awareness of particular political issues and their work has included social comment as well as visual statements about their chosen medium. David Poston, for example, protested against the poor working conditions and exploitation of the black miners in South Africa by exhibiting in 1975 a forged-steel neckpiece, shaped like a manacle and with the words "Diamonds, gold and slavery are forever" inlaid in

The collar and arm-ring (1986), made by Darani Lewers and Helge Larsen, shows how jewellers have used body adornment as a sculptural response to the human form. The chemically coloured gilding metal shows a technological development that is influencing colour and texture in jewellery.

silver. Some simply rejected the use of precious metals and gemstones because of their high cost and the elitism they represented.

Australia is now beginning to establish a jewellery style of its own. During the 1960s and 70s many European jewellers visited, conducting workshops and exhibiting their work there. Initially this led to a spate of derivative work from the newly graduating students which fed an existing trade invariably run by immigrants from Europe. However, the seeds had been sown and students began to experiment with jewellery as a means of self expression. Soon jewellers emerged with a distinctive Australian feel. Wolf Wennrich, Helge Larsen and Darani Lewers have been the key figures in this development while Frank Bauer, who trained in Germany, Anne Brownsworth, Susan Cohn, Rowena Gough, Peter Tully and Lyn Tune are just a few of the new generation of Australian jewellers producing increasingly interesting results.

In the 1970s imagery from space hardware and micro-technology was captured in jewellery form by Pierre Degen (a Swiss now working in the UK), the Austrian Fritz Maierhofer and the Englishman Roger Morris. They used metal and coloured plastics in combination, with finishes that were reminiscent of machine-made products. The forms sometimes seemed more concerned with the sculptural than the wearable and had enough presence to stand alone. Roger Morris even made sculptural pieces which included jewellery within them that could then be taken out and worn.

In Holland, Bakker and Leersum rejected precious metals and used metals previously associated with indus-trial manufacture instead. Their idea was to show that even if a metal is neither rare nor expensive it can have aesthetic qualities. They were also continuing the Bauhaus tradition of gearing their designs for mass-production.

The idealistic notion that "good" and "innovative" design could be made available to all was taken up by various jewellers. However, manufacturers have remained steadfastly resistant to taking risks, so this has remained an ideal rather than a reality. Innovative jewellers also create their own elitism, however unwittingly, through a pre-ciousness in style rather than materials. Despite this, there is little doubt that the innovators have influenced the more commercial end of costume jewellery – which makes the originals the more collectable.

The use of different materials, from platinum to paper, has brought infinite variety into the world of jewellery. And space technology has contributed materials, as well as imagery, to jewellery design – particularly the refractory metals ranging from niobium, which is the same density as gold, to titanium, which is very light and strong. But their most interesting property is that they are capable of chang-ing their surface until they reflect every colour of the spec-trum. Edward de Large, now working in the USA, was one

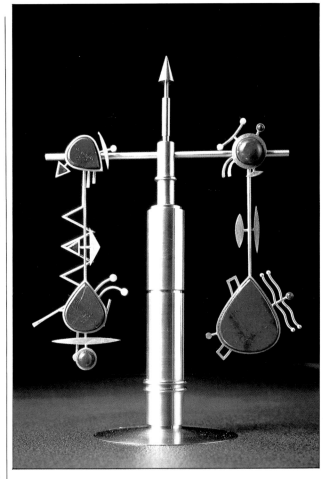

of the first to perfect the use of refractory metals for jewellery, creating beautiful illusionistic landscapes on brooches and pendants.

The Style and Post-Modernism

Today's jewellers are again reflecting cultural trends, using the pluralism associated with Post-Modern culture to widen their scope. The political aspects of jewellery have diminished. Decoration without an added meaning is acceptable again.

A greater element of fun has also crept into body adorn-ment. The Englishman Geoff Roberts, formerly a student of sculpture and printmaking, works with plastic and brightly coloured metal foil to produce deliberately cheap jewellery that is essentially a combination of fun and fantasy. The Swiss Otto Kunzli, who studied under Hermann Jünger in Munich, uses a more satirical wit with such things as large three-dimensional brooches covered in "tasteless" wall-paper. And fine artist Peter Chang has hit the headlines with his large, brightly coloured bangles in vacuum-formed plastic. Only time will tell how they will endure.

Sculptural objects that become jewellery or jewellery that becomes sculpture are results of the jewellery revolution of the 1960s and 70s. Wendy Ramshaw is notable for her sculptural stands that displayed her ring sets. She began making stands for her jewellery in the 1970s and this earring stand from 1988 shows that her ideas and forms continue to develop and intrigue the viewer.

INFLUENCES

1

2

3

Movements in fine art inevitably affect experimental jewellers, and the Minimalist sculptors who emerged in the 1970s had their counterparts among jewellers, particularly in Holland. Forms were refined and simplified to the extreme, occasionally using repetition to add power and emphasis, as with the galvanized iron and clear plexiglas sculpture (1) by Donald Judd from 1985. Dutch jeweller Herman Hermsen has reduced his neckpiece (2) to one clear dynamic line, but with subtle changes of curve to give it a three-dimensional quality.

A fascinating correlation can be seen between the work of jewellers like Lam de Wolf from Holland (4) and traditional tribal jewellery (3). Jewellers who create total body adornments seem to be expressing a basic human need for ritual and symbolic ceremony that is nowadays lacking in our lives. The beautiful Masai woman wears jewellery that is exciting and joyful, a real celebration of life and beauty, but it is also very complex. It must have taken many careful hours, not only to make, but also to put on.

5

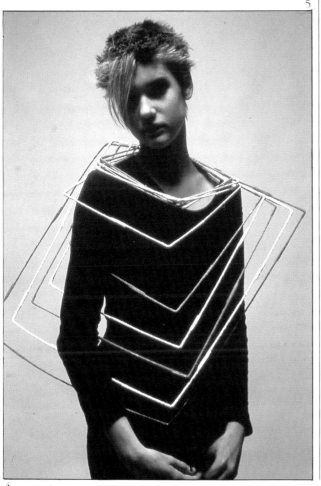

4

One of the themes of youth culture of the early 1960s was the future seen as some kind of science-fiction adventure. Space-age clothing, pioneered by Courrèges, materialized from Paris. The "Cosmos" dress from Balmain (6) in 1967 exhibited the trend towards simple geometric shapes and shorter hemlines. Friedrich Becker's kinetic jewellery illustrated the same geometric dynamism. He started introducing parts that moved in response to the wearer in 1965. The white-gold and diamond bangle (5) dates from 1970.

6

MAINSTREAM MODERN

1

2

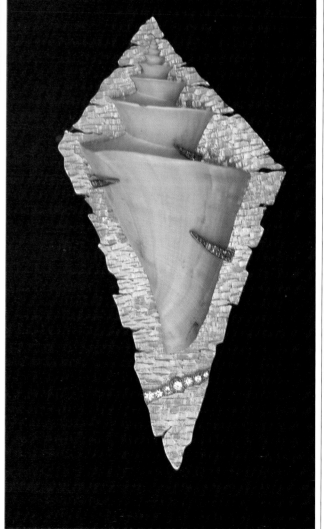

3

Andrew Grima (born 1921) has developed his own original approach to designing jewellery (3). Although he has adopted the contemporary trend for texture, abstract shapes and even the use of objets trouvés, he creates an extravagant and opulent end product. The British royal family have bought his jewels both for themselves and for State gifts.

David Thomas (born 1938) set up his own workshop in the 1960s after studying at the Royal College of Art in London. Working instinctively, he liked to build up his pieces organically rather than by designing in detail on paper first. He made pieces like the swirling gold wire and diamond brooch (4) piece by piece, soldering with a micro-welder.

New jewellers in the 1960s designed for the mainstream gold and diamond market, but developed innovative ideas. Charles de Temple came from an unusual background; although he now lives in London his father was Tom Mix, the famous American cowboy. His jewellery was equally unconventional. His wedding rings (1) exemplify his encrusted and heavily textured finishes. John Donald's brooch with rutilated quartz (2) shows his inventive use of gold in a surround that seems to continue in a natural crystalline form from the stone.

4

5

6

The geometry of the 1960s is noticeably more hard-edged than that of Art Deco designs. The brooch (**5**) by Gillian Packard, in different coloured golds with emeralds and diamonds, has more to do with the bas relief pictures of someone like Ben Nicholson than with traditional jewellery ornamentation. Gillian Packard, born in 1938, was a graduate of the Royal College of Art in London. She is better known for her rings, which were often sensually curving and easy to wear. Her ingenious wedding and engagement ring sets would neatly slot together, a style that many were to emulate.

Björn Weckström's impressive necklace (**6**) uses gold with supreme confidence. The bold, nuggety segments have no need of gemstones. Weckström was born in Helsinki in 1935 and worked for the famous Lapponia Jewellery company there. He now has his own gallery also in Helsinki and belongs to the Finnish Sculptors' Union as well as ORNAMO, the designers' union. There is an increasing acceptance that jewellers can be sculptors and vice-versa, although resistance from the more traditional art academies is vehement.

NON-CONFORMISM

The most influential jeweller working in Britain in the 1950s was Gerda Flockinger. Although there were changing attitudes in America and other parts of Europe, whereby jewellers presented their work as art, Britain demonstrated a more traditional approach and few jewellers were prepared to step outside the bounds of acceptability. Flockinger inspired many of the new generation of experimental jewellers not just with her technical approach, but with her attitude towards jewellery design and making. Born in 1927 in Innsbruck, she studied fine art at St Martin's School of Art in London from 1945 to 50. She then went on to study at the Central School of Art and Design from 1950 to 55, where she took up jewellery as well as etching and enamelling. She was one of the first jewellers to be given a one-person exhibition at the Arnolfini Gallery in Bristol, signifying an important step in jewellery development. It

1983 cufflinks in silver, 18-carat gold, diamonds and cultured pearls.

was as a result of the work, attitudes and personalities of jewellers like Gerda Flockinger that it became usual for jewellery to be seen in galleries and in exhibitions.

When she inaugurated a jewellery course at Hornsey College of Art (now Middlesex Polytechnic) in London in 1962, she had a more direct influence on new jewellers. The course was exciting and experimental and Middlesex is still considered an important and prestigious place to study. David

Poston and Charlotte de Syllas both studied with her. David Poston used his work to express his political views in the early 1970s, while Charlotte de Syllas developed a profound independence from familiar trends. It is noticeable that they each found a unique means of self-expression, no doubt helped by their college environment.

2

*The bangle and earrings (**1**) show Gerda Flockinger's individual style, with adeptly melted metal sheet and fused lines of wire. The bangle (1973) is made from silver and pearls and the earrings (1975) are intricately constructed of silver with oxides and 18-carat gold. She has subtly included small brilliant-cut diamonds in the earrings, and finished them with hanging pearls.*

*Elisabeth Holder's technical excellence reflects her German training. Born in Sindelfingen in West Germany in 1950 she undertook an apprenticeship training as well as college study. She came to London and studied again at the Royal College of Art, finally setting up her workshop in London in 1980. Her brooch (1988) shows a masterly use of metals, with a typically elegant and simple but expressive design that stretches out and ends with a flourish (**2**).*

1

3

4

5

Many British jewellers in the 1970s abandoned precious metals in favour of other materials. Catherine Mannheim has stayed with metal, but not with tradition. She has used the imagery of Pop art – words spelt out in raised letters, figurative pictures, and sometimes photographs framed behind glass – for a brooch. Her amphora brooch (**4**) is fused silver with applied gold (1986).

Jewellery in the past was often related to myth, magic and ceremony, and the work of Tone Vigeland seems to echo the Nordic traditions of such symbolic and efficacious jewellery. She was born in Oslo in 1938, studying at the Kunst & Handverksskolen there from 1955 and at Oslo Yrkesskole from 1957. She established her own workshop in 1961. The dramatic and feather-like necklace (**3**) is made from silver, steel and gold with mother-of-pearl in the clasp (1983).

Hand-worked metal, made with the mind, the hand and the heart can create the fetish objects of our urban age. The symbolism is timeless, and the jewellery is essentially precious and compelling. Cynthia Cousens's hatpins (**5**) in copper, gold, steel and silver are very much more than the sum of their parts or merely the result of technical skill.

NON-CONFORMISM

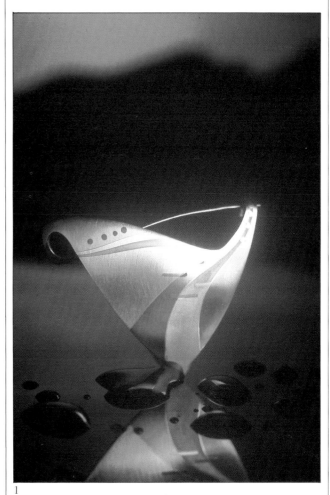

1

Refractory metals provided a new resource for jewellers in the 20th century. Their potential for vivid colours has made them very popular. Anne Marie Shillitoe was one of the pioneers in their use in the UK. Unlike the majority of exponents she uses them with subtlety in elegant curving forms. The fibula (1) is in anodized titanium inlaid with tantalum and niobium, c.1980.

William Harper follows his American jewellery pioneers in seeing his work as art. "The White Hermaphrodite" (2) is a brooch relating to his theme of the search for beauty and truth through dichotomy. He posits the idea that the perfect human would be both male and female. To create life takes a male and female and to make art one must also be both.

2

Australian jewellery in the 19th century used images of local flora and fauna. Helge Larsen and Darani Lewers have reflected this celebration of their surroundings with their "Kookaburra" pendant (3). They have been pioneers of the modern jewellery movement in Australia since 1961. They feel that their jewellery is a form of body language through which they can express their ideas and feelings. When worn it can take on further meaning from the personality of the wearer.

3

5

Sometimes the concept behind a piece of jewellery is more important than the finished piece. Gijs Bakker (born 1942 in Holland) has consistently managed to surprise even the most experimental. The necklace (4) of flower petals, which by nature are temporary and insubstantial, are preserved for posterity inside a carefully constructed spiral – man's attempts to control nature perhaps?

The highly personal nature of jewellery has been taken to an extreme by Gerd Rothman (born 1941 in Germany) who has cast small parts of individual people's bodies in silver. The earring (5) was made in 1984.

4

ABSTRACT AND NON-PRECIOUS PIECES

1

Fritz Maierhofer (born 1941 in Austria) is another jeweller noted for his precision pieces. He admits to being more concerned with structure and form than with wearability, although this does not mean they are not worn. In this recent girder-like pin (**3**), he has contrasted shiny yellow metal with oxidized white metal.

3

2

4

Frank Bauer (born in 1942 in Germany and now living in Australia) reveals his architectural background in his beautifully constructed geometric pieces. The cube earrings (**1**) are in 18-carat gold (1980). Joel Degen (born in 1941 in France, now living in London) shows his methods of construction in his 1980s wedding and engagement rings (**2**).

David Watkins (born 1940) is one of the leading contemporary jewellers in Britain. He has consistently produced impressive, sculptural collections of jewellery, the later pieces being made from steel coated with coloured neoprene. These necklaces can be worn separately or in combination (**4**).

David Poston (born 1948) has moved through various stages of development. He was one of the first jewellers to include textiles in his work, and caused a commotion when he made a huge necklace out of stones for an elephant! His later work has been very simple and refined like the neckpieces and bangles (1983) in steel and titanium (**5**).

5

Wendy Ramshaw (born 1939) is one of the most successful contemporary jewellers to have emerged out of the 1970s. She has managed to combine fashion and innovation in her work, and her award-winning designs have proved to be extremely popular with the buying public. She first became known for her ring sets which she presented on rocket-shaped stands. She turned the stands and parts of the rings on a lathe, but maintained a quality of feminine prettiness within her high-tech imagery. Although she has predominantly and skilfully used precious metals, she has also experimented with paper, glass, porcelain and even developed "performance art" pieces. The "Orbit" necklaces pictured here (6) were made in 1988.

6

COLOUR AND FASHION

Fashion jewellers can often be freer and more spontaneous with their jewellery. The materials are cheaper and more easily marketed. Katzie Hughes screen-prints on to paper and then embeds the paper in resin. With processes like these she can be more experimental with her shapes and colours (*2*).

1

2

3

High-fashion jewellery is also now the province of the artist–jeweller. Peter Chang is primarily a fine artist, but his vacuum-formed plastic jewellery was recently used by Rifat Ozbeck for a fashion show. The bangles (*1* and *3*) are good examples of his dramatic and highly decorative creations.

Geoff Roberts is one of the most prolific and inventive fashion jewellers. He initially trained as a sculptor and then as a printmaker. His acrylic necklace (*4*) hints at the colour, intensity and preciousness of gems with the rich colours obtained from metal blocking foil.

4

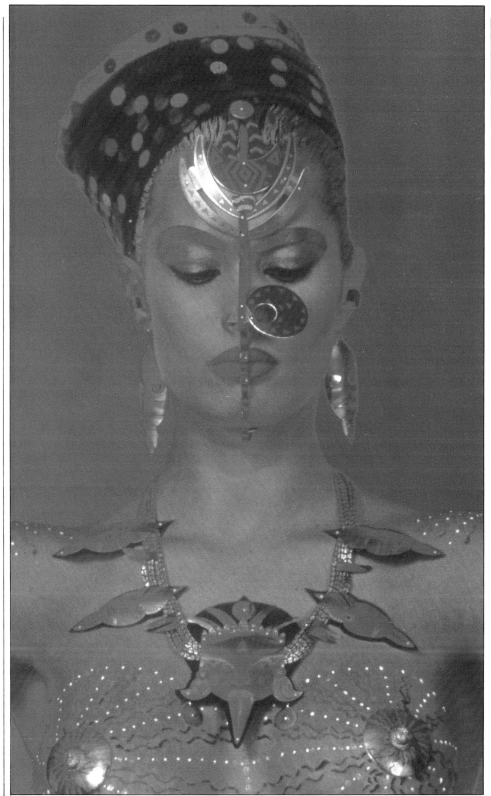

Titanium is a hard metal to fashion, but Clarissa (**5**) has managed to achieve great delicacy in her work. Her exotic imagery stems from her research in Indonesia, although her work has always involved complex colour patterns and interesting shapes. During her studies at the Royal College of Art she experimented with coating different surfaces with an iridescent titanium colour.

After the street style of Punk, it no longer seemed excessive to swathe oneself with paste jewels and strings of pearls. At a time when the British public were hungry for glamour Monty Don brought out a range of large crystal and pearl drops topped with ribbon bows. Many more sumptuous designs followed. Current work includes large, glittering paste hanging baskets (**6**).

6

5

WEARABLE ART

Artist–jewellers sometimes include objects that relate to their jewellery alongside their wearable work largely by their scale and preciousness. Onno Boekhoudt (born 1944 in Holland) produced this group of objects (**1**) in 1984. He has proved to be an influential force in Dutch jewellery. He has shown a less clinical and altogether freer approach than that of his Minimalist contemporaries. He teaches at the Gerrit Rietveld Akademie in Amsterdam, Holland's most prestigious design school.

1

2

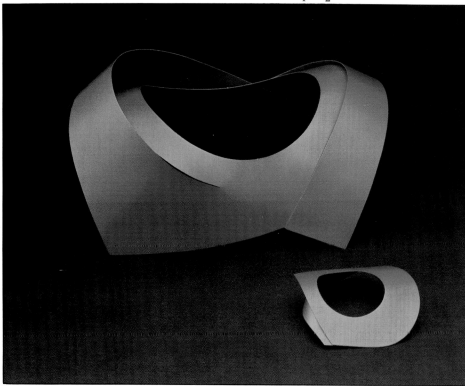

3

Susannah Heron (born 1949 in England) has proved to be one of the most thoughtful and inventive jewellers in the UK. As she moved towards more sculptural forms she called her work "Wearables" rather than jewellery. Her "Wearable: large turquoise and red hat" from 1982 (**2**) heralded her complete move from jewellery to sculpture.

Although some jewellery can stand on its own as sculpture, most sculptural pieces are still only really completed when they are placed on the human body. Helge Larsen and Darani Lewer's anodized aluminium collar and armring from 1986 (**3**) powerfully suggest the curves of the body and anticipate a wearer.

4

Peter Tully (born 1949) is an Australian who has developed an expressive, flamboyant and witty style that speaks volumes about his native country. A large exhibition of Australian jewellery that toured Europe in the early 1980s included his "Australian Belt" which consisted of brightly coloured acrylic cutouts of Australian maps covered with cutout Vegemite labels, kangaroos and Sydney Opera House. "Urban Tribalwear" (1981), is made from fluorescent vinyls, plastics and rubber and comprises a head-dress, breastplate, necklaces, bags, armbands and a skirt (4).

Gijs Bakker's is a more disturbing and calculated wit. His design techniques are cool and precise, but the end results can be startling. His idea of laminating photographs in clear plastic makes for a frighteningly realistic illusion (5). The necklace shown is entitled "Embracement" and dates from 1982.

When jewellery attempts to be witty it usually does so in a subtle and abstract way. But some jewellers exhibit their wit more overtly. Otto Kunzli (born in 1948 in Switzerland) studied metalwork in Zürich and jewellery in Munich under Hermann Jünger. His excellent training gives him all the more scope to subvert traditional jewellery values. His wit and ingenuity are matched by his craft and design skills. His dislike of jewellery as a status symbol or investment is epitomized in his replica of a gold bar made from cardboard (6).

6

5

181

FIGURATIVE WORK

Figurative jewellery will never lose its appeal. Forms that are easily recognized can stir the emotions in an immediate and direct way. Charlotte de Syllas has never followed a particular trend with her jewellery and often works for many months on one piece so that when it finally leaves her hands it is exquisitely crafted and quite unique. The "Magpie" necklace (**1**) is made from black nephrite and white jadeite. The secondary feathers and tail are labradorite laminated on to black nephrite. The kumihimo silk braids are by Catherine Martin.

1

American jewellers are often uninhibited by design "traditions" and produce work that is idiosyncratic and expressive of its maker's personality. Richard Mawdsley's narrative belt buckle (2), in sterling silver, lapis lazuli

and coral (1976), is entitled "Goneril, Regan, Cordelia". It combines the look of instrument parts and an expressionistic female form almost in the traditions of assemblage art. His virtuosity is particularly evident in

his "Feast" bracelet (1974), which is a perfect miniature of a table laid with jugs, goblets, dishes of food, wine buckets and cutlery.

Sophie Chell shows a cooler, more British-influenced approach with her half jackets (3). Taking male stereotypes she reduces them to brooch form with clever craft skills. Her brooches from 1980 utilize silver, silver-gilt and niobium,

materials with qualities that can be manipulated to represent particular images rather than to celebrate the materials themselves.

2

3

Bruno Martinazzi (born 1923 in Italy) is another artist who combines sculpture and jewellery. He originally studied chemistry and then psychology, before attending the State School of Art in Florence. His "Goldfinger" bracelet (4) dates from 1969. Viliama Grakalic (who was born in 1942 in Yugoslavia and moved to Australia in 1963) constantly uses the human form in her jewellery.

Her "Falling Man" brooch (5) is from a series of three.

4

5

TOWARD THE FUTURE

Robert Ebendorf's feelings towards his jewellery are characteristic of many other artist—jewellers working in the 1980s. He explains that he wants to spark energy with his visual effects. He wants to encompass in his jewellery aspects of the life and culture that surround him; the experiences that we are all responding to in different ways. He wants to use his learned craft skills as a means to an end—to explore his creative potential—and make his finished work an expressive means of communication.

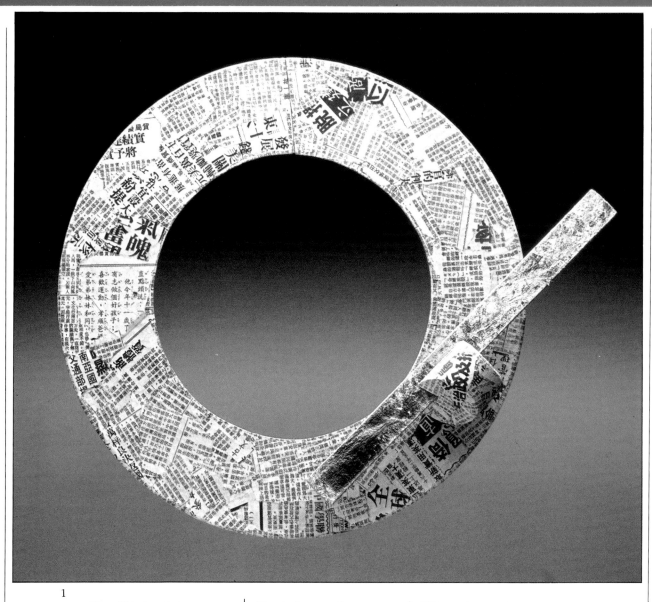

1

Two of his recent pieces are shown here. The neck-ring (**1**) measures 25cm (10in) in diameter and is constructed in an old Chinese newspaper and 24-carat gold foil. The mixed media necklace (**2**) is the same diameter; the beads are 5cm (2in) across.
Born in Kansas, USA in 1938

Ebendorf received his Master's degree in the fine arts. He has spent time in Norway studying and working at Norway Silver Design. He is currently Professor of Art at the State University of New York. Ebendorf is also a founding member and past President of the Society of North American Goldsmiths and in

1982 was honoured as a Distinguished Member of the Society.

2

GLOSSARY

Acanthus: ornament based on the leaves of the Mediterranean Acanthus plant. Originally used to decorate the capitals of Corinthian columns.

Acrylic: a plastic resin used by some contemporary jewellers since the 1960s. It can be moulded and cut, has a wide colour range and is sometimes used in conjunction with metals.

Agate: a variety of CHALCEDONY, usually banded, in various coloured layers alternating with milky white. Also MOSS-AGATE: a translucent grey, with green, black or red inclusions of various oxides.

Aigrette (Fr.): a vertical hair ornament, usually jewelled, in the form of a plume of feathers or a spray of flowers.

Alexandrite: a type of CHRYSOBERYL discovered in the Urals in 1831, and named after Tsar Alexander II. Occurs in red, white and green forms and is extremely light-sensitive, sometimes changing colour from deep green to bright red.

Amazonstone (amazonite): a FELDSPAR varying from bright to bluish-green, it is opaque with an iridescent sheen. It cleaves easily, so is unsuitable for faceting and is usually cut EN CABOCHON.

Baguette (Fr.): a method of cutting gemstones in the shape of a long narrow rectangle bordered by four step-cut FACETS.

Bakelite: the trade name for the first thermosetting resin, patented in 1910 by the Belgian, Dr Leo Baekeland. Used for the manufacture of early records, plastic wares, telephones etc.

Balas ruby (also **spinel ruby**): misnomers for a spinel whose colour resembles a ruby. The spinel is a bright transparent gemstone which occurs in many colours.

Baroque pearl: a large misshapen pearl, caused by an oyster pearl formation around an irregularly shaped inclusion.

Bas-relief: when the relief, or projection from a surface, is low or shallow.

Basse-taille (Fr.): an enamelling technique in which translucent enamels are introduced over a ground which has been chased, engraved or otherwise worked to create a modelled surface. The enamel colour varies in intensity with the depth of the cutting.

Berlin Iron: originally early 19th century cast-iron jewellery from the Berlin Iron Foundry. Most of it was produced in the period 1812-15 when pieces were presented in exchange for gold jewellery donated to the war-effort during the Napoleonic Wars. Some was also made in France.

Bezel: the principal component of a decorative finger ring, it surmounts the hoop encircling the finger. Term also used for the setting for a central stone or decoration.

Bijouterie (Fr.): a term which distinguishes jewellery made of gold and enamels from JOAILLERIE (Fr.) which is composed mainly of gemstones.

Biliment: a row of stones or pearls which bordered or transversed "gable" headdresses or French hoods in 16th century England.

Blister pearl: an uneven, sometimes hollow pearl, with a raw underside which is usually hidden in a setting.

Bodkin: a long ornamental hairpin, of gold or silver set with gems; fashionable for fastening hair in the Renaissance.

Bracteate: a term for a thin sheet of gold applied to pieces of jewellery, coins, medals etc.

Brilliant cut: a method of gem-cutting in which the upper part of the stone is cut in as many as 33 FACETS, and the lower part in 25. Particularly suited to diamonds.

Cabochon (Fr.): a stone with a smooth, curved, highly polished and unfaceted surface. The oldest method of gem-cutting still in use.

Calibré-cut (Fr.): a method of cutting usually small gemstones, to fit closely into groups or clusters which are massed around a main stone. Often an oblong or elliptical cut.

Cameo: a gem, hardstone or shell, of which the upper section is carved in relief while the lower serves as a ground.

Cannetille (Fr.): A particular type of FILIGREE used on jewellery settings, incorporating shells and burr-like motifs. Popular in France during the first half of the 19th century.

Carbuncle: almandine garnet cut en cabochon

Carcanet: bands of jewels worn as necklaces.

Cat's Eye: a general term for several varieties of gemstone which, in certain lights when cut en cabochon, exhibit a luminous moving line bisecting the stone. This is most notable in the lustrous yellowish-brown variety of CHRYSOBERYL.

Celluloid: the generic term for Pyroxylin (cellulose nitrate) plastics pioneered in Britain, but finally patented in America c. 1870 by the brothers James and Isaiah Hyatt.

Chalcedony: a variety of QUARTZ, usually of pale milky blue or grey, and evenly coloured. It is porous so can be easily dyed to enhance or alter its colour. Its several gemstone varieties include: AGATE, SARDONYX, CORNELIAN, CHRYSPOPRASE, ONYX.

Champlevé enamel (Fr.): an enamelling technique in which individual compartments are created to receive the enamel by cutting away troughs or "cells" in the background metal. The enamel is then polished down to the level of the metal cells, forming a design.

Chaplet: a medieval hair ornament in the form of an encircling band of ornamental gold flowers and gemstones.

Chatelaine (Fr.): a decorative hook worn at the waist, from which are suspended on hooks or chains, various items for practical daily use in the household.

Chrysoberyl: said to derive from the Greek *chrysos* (gold) because of its typically golden-yellow colour; it can vary to yellowish and bluish-green and brown. The most attractive and sought-after examples are the ALEXANDRTE and CAT'S EYE.

Chrysoprase: a variety of QUARTZ which occurs in shades of deep to yellowish-green and is usually cut en cabochon.

Citrine: the correct name for all yellow and pale brown varieties of QUARTZ and the most common yellow stone available.

Cloisonné enamel (Fr.): an enamelling technique where compartments or *cloisons* are built up from the metal background by attaching metal strips at right-angles to it. The *cloisons* are then filled in with enamel leaving their tops exposed.

Collet: band of metal encircling a stone and holding it in place.

Collier de Chien (Fr.): or Dog Collar: a choker of many strands usually of pearls or diamonds, sometimes with a central brooch or *plaque-de-cou*. A fashion popularized by Queen Alexandra.

Coque de Perle (Fr.): a large, thin section cut from the central whorl of a shell of the Nautilus. It is irregularly shaped, very white and resembles somewhat the BLISTER PEARL.

Cornelian: a translucent reddish CHALCEDONY. Perhaps due to its fleshy colour it is also known as CARNELIAN, from *carnis* (L. flesh).

Coronal: a simple open crown worn by Medieval noblemen and women, it is usually decorated with *fleurons*.

Cosse de Pois (Fr.): a decorative motif consisting of a repeated design of elongated leaf-shapes resembling pea-pods. Originated in France in the early 17th century.

Crocidolite: a fibrous mineral, its colour ranges from mauve to green. When decomposed as quartz it can change to a golden brown, which is known as a TIGER'S EYE.

Email en ronde bosse (Fr.): a type of painted enamelling in which the enamel is applied to figures or other modelling in high relief. Also known as encrusted enamelling.

En plein (Fr.): when enamel is applied directly to a surface rather than to plaques attached to it.

En tremblant (Fr.): in which parts of large, ornamental, usually floral, jewels are set on tiny springs which quiver or "tremble" when worn.

Esclavage (Fr.): literally, slavery; a necklace comprising three chains or strings of jewels or beads which are equidistant.

Feldspar: the name for a large group of minerals. Though of geological importance, few are suitable for gemstones. These include MOONSTONE and AMAZONSTONE.

Ferronière (Fr.): a hair ornament in the form of a chain encircling the head, with a pendant which falls at the centre of the forehead.

Filigree: delicate silver or gold wire threads designed in complex repeating patterns.

Foil: an ancient means of improving the colour and brilliance of stones by backing them with a thin leaf of highly polished metal.

Fret: a geometrical ornament of intersecting horizontal and vertical lines repeated to form a pattern.

Garnet: a gemstone popular from antiquity, the name derives from *granatum* (L.) for pomegranate, a reference to its colour. Its six varieties include: ALMANDINE: dark crimson in colour and often cut en cabochon, when it is known as a CARBUNCLE; DEMANTOID: green in colour, its name refers to its diamond-like sparkle, it is often used as a series of tiny stones surrounding a larger gem; and HESSONITE: transparent yellow, orange or brownish in colour. Also known as "cinnamon stone" and "jacinth".

Giardinetto (It.): literally, small garden: a type of late 17th to 18th century ring of openwork floral design, set with various coloured gems.

Gimmel: derived from *gemellus* (L. a twin): the name for a ring which separates into two interlinked parts.

Girandole: a type of earring or brooch in which three pendant drops are suspended from a larger bow-shaped setting.

Granulation: An Etruscan gold-working technique, revived in the 19th century, in which minute grains of gold are applied to a metal surface forming patterns in low relief.

Greek cross: a cross with four equidistant arms of equal size.

Hardstone: a loose term generally applied to opaque semi- or non-precious stones.

Intaglio: the opposite of CAMEO, in which a design is carved into the surface of a gemstone or hardstone.

Jasper: closely related to AGATE, its many impurities cause its coloration of red, brown, yellow or green. It is more common than CHALCEDONY and a popular stone for carving.

Jerusalem cross: a cross with four equidistant and equally sized arms which terminate in flanged ends.

Joaillerie (Fr.): see BIJOUTERIE

Lapis Lazuli: a complex mineral of an intense purply-blue, sometimes with inclusions of sparkling pyrites. Widely used for decoration and ornament. Because of its colour and resistance to fading, it was also ground for use as a pigment for the paint colour Ultramarine. The name possibly originated in the Middle Ages, "lapis" meaning stone and "lazuli" derived from the Arabic word for blue.

Latin cross: a cross with four arms in which the shorter transverse member crosses the upright one third from the top.

Lemel: the floor sweepings of precious metals from a jeweller's workshop.

Malachite: a copper carbonate mineral banded alternately bright and dark green. As it polishes well and is opaque it is excellent for carved flat brooches, pendants and beads, and for a large variety of objects and vessels.

Maltese cross: a cross with four arms of equal length and size, which widen as they extend from the centre.

Marcasite: the trade name given to the tiny bright metallic stones called iron pyrites,

when used in jewellery.

Memento Mori: for "Remember you must die". Jewellery intended as a reminder and warning of death, and reflecting this late 16th and 17th century preoccupation; featuring skulls and crossbones, skeletons and coffins.

Moonstone: a silvery blue translucent stone generally cut en cabochon to display its silky sheen to best advantage.

Mussel pearls: or "River Pearls", produced by the freshwater mussel *Unio* found in some rivers of Europe and in the Mississippi Basin. Inferior to the oyster pearl.

Niobium: a rare, lustrous grey metal, similar in appearance to TITANIUM, though heavier and more expensive. Was extensively explored in the UK Nuclear Energy programme. It is malleable and ductile so can be hand-worked, and this, together with its rich coloration on heating, has made it a popular metal with some jewellers today.

Obsidian: dark, glassy volcanic rock formed by rapid solidification of lava.

Onyx: a variety of CHALCEDONY, it is layered in shades of black and white, thus lending itself to cameo-cutting, the upper section forming a contrast with the lower.

Palmette: a fan-shaped decorative motif resembling a palm leaf.

Parkesine: the first polymer to be used commercially as a plastic and forerunner of CELLULOID. The invention of Alexander Parkes, it was introduced at the Great International Exhibition in London in 1862.

Parure (Fr.): a suite of matching jewellery. Also DEMI-PARURE, usually of two matching pieces only, e.g. necklace and earrings.

Paste: glass, usually containing lead oxide, which is used to resemble gemstones.

Pâte de Verre (Fr.): a glass-making technique in which crushed glass is made into a paste, coloured with metallic oxides and fused. It is then moulded and fired and the resulting glass is dense and opaque with a frosty surface.

Pavé, (pavé-set) (Fr.): a "paving" of stones, where a number of small stones are set so closely together that the only discernible fixing is the small metal grains which hold each stone in place.

Peridot: a transparent green gemstone popular since antiquity, it has a distinctive "oily" lustre and has been used ceremonially in the past instead of emeralds.

Pinchbeck: an alloy of copper and zinc intended to simulate gold. Invented by the watchmaker Christopher Pinchbeck in the 18th century and used for making cheaper jewellery set with pastes or inexpensive stones.

Platinum: recently discovered strong, silvery-white metal. It is more expensive than gold, neither corrodes nor tarnishes, but is very heavy. It has been used for jewellery since the 19th century.

Plique-à-Jour (Fr.): a technique of translucent enamelling which, as it has no metal backing, allows light to travel through (hence *à jour*). The enamel is supported by a network of wire cells and the effect is similar to stained glass.

Point cut: a polished diamond in its natural, octahedron, form. This very early style was superseded by later fashions.

Quartz: from *querertz* (Ger: "crossing ore") a reference to its tendency to run across other mineral veins. The most common of minerals, it is mostly crystalline. There are three varieties and many colours. See also ROCK CRYSTAL.

Reliquary: a richly decorated vessel or receptacle for a relic pertaining to the life or person of Christ or the saints.

Rhinestone: a type of ROCK CRYSTAL used as an inexpensive substitute for diamonds.

Rivière: a necklace consisting of single matched or graduated stones, usually diamonds.

Rock crystal: quartz in its natural state and quite colourless.

Rosary or Decade ring: a ring with 10 projections for counting the number of "Aves" to be said in each decade of the Rosary.

Rose-cut: a method of gemstone cutting with a flat base and a large number of triangular facets rising to a point.

Sardonyx: an ONYX banded alternately white and reddish-brown (Sard), often used for cameos and seals.

Sautoir (Fr.): a long necklace or chain sometimes enamelled or jewelled, often worn diagonally across the body from shoulder to hip, or looped up and pinned to the bodice or waistband. Also used to suspend spectacles or a watch.

Semi-Precious stones: a term generally used to refer to all gemstones other than the PRECIOUS ones of diamond, ruby, emerald, sapphire and pearl.

Sodalite: a mineral resembling LAPIS LAZULI of which it is a component. It is also used as a gemstone in its own right.

Scarab: a type of beetle revered by the ancient Egyptians and used by them as an ornamental device, and for jewellery.

Scotch Pebble: the popular 19th century name for the local Scottish AGATES and other HARDSTONES set into jewellery.

Table-cut: a method of gemcutting in which a square or rectangular "table" is cut on both the top and the bottom, the lower being smaller, and with four facets sloping upwards and downwards from the central "girdle".

Tiger's Eye: see CROCIDOLITE

Tinctured Doublet: a composite stone comprising a layer of a precious stone cemented to a layer of an inferior one, which is also "tinctured" or dyed.

Titanium: a metallic element discovered in 1789, and used principally in aerospace technology. Now favoured by some jewellers for the subtle and attractive range of colours it acquires when heated. It is also lightweight and durable.

Topaz: the so-called "yellow stone" which also occurs in a range of browns and as pale aquamarine. The rare pink variety (mostly obtained by heat treatment of brown stones) is highly prized.

Torc: a type of metal neck ring or armlet in the shape of an open hoop, often with ornamental terminals. Generally associated with Celtic jewellery.

Tourmaline: from the Sinhalese root meaning "coloured stone", it possesses the widest colour range of all the gemstones, resulting from its complex chemical composition. It can also be parti-coloured.

Vinaigrette: a small decorative receptacle containing a sponge saturated in scented vinegar intended as an emergency treatment for faintness. Often worn on a chain suspended from a bracelet.

Yellow sapphire: sometimes known as "Oriental Topaz", it is a less valuable variety of the transparent "Corundum" of which the various blue sapphires are the most prized. Its colour is due to ferric oxide.

187

INDEX

INDEX

CREDITS

Abbreviations used:

BM = By Courtesy of the Trustees of the British Museum. V&A = By Courtesy of The Board and Trustees of the Victoria & Albert Museum. WFA = Werner Forman Archive

p12/13, BM; p14, WFA/BM; p15, BM; p16, BM; p18, 1. Jack Ogden, 2. The Harry Smith Horticultural Photographic Collection, 3. BM, 4. Ashmolean Museum, Oxford; p19, 5. WFA, 6. WFA/Cairo Museum, 7. BM; p20, BM; p21, WFA, 4. The Metropolitan Museum of Art, Fletcher Fund, 1947, 5. BM; p22, BM; p23, 4. BM, 6. WFA/The Metropolitan Museum of Art, 5. BM; p24, BM; p25, 3. WFA/Hermitage Museum, Leningrad, 4. WFA/ National Museum of Ireland, Dublin, 5. WFA/BM; p26, photo Jack Ogden 2. BM, 3. BM; p27, 4. photo Jack Ogden 5. WFA; p28, 1. WFA/Statens Historiska Museet, Stockholm, box BM, 2. photo, Jack Ogden; p29, 3. Brooklyn Museum, 4. photo, Jack Ogden 5. Jack Ogden; p30, 1. & 2. WFA/Statens Historiska Museet, Stockholm, 3. WFA/Universitetets Oldsaksamling, Oslo, p31, 4. WFA/Universitetets Oldsaksamling, Oslo, 5. & 6. WFA/Statens Historiska Museet, Stockholm; p32, Allerheiligen Museum, Schaffhausen, p34, Statens Historiska Museet/Antikvarisk-Topografiska, Arkivet, Stockholm; p35, Musée du Louvre, Paris; p37, Domschatzkammer, Essen/photo Pieter Happel p38, 1. The Cleveland Museum of Art, John Hartington Art and Polytechnic Trust, 30, 742, 2. Architectural Association Slide Library; p39, 3-4, Kunstgewerbe Museum, East Berlin, 5. WFA/ Biblioteca Nazionale Marciana, Venice; p40, 1. Landesmuseum, Mainz, 2. Nationalmuseet Copenhagen/photo Niels Elswing; p41, 3, Archivo Mas, Barcelona, 4, V&A; p42, Statens Historiska Museet, Stockholm; p43, 2, Museo de Castelvecchio, Verona/SCALA, 3, BM, 4, National Museums of Scotland, Edinburgh; p44-45, 1, Musée Cluny, Paris, 2, National Gallery, London, 3, Schatzkammer, Munich, 4, Domschatzkammer, Aachen/photo Ann Münchow; p46, 1, BM, 2, Museo Nazionale (Bargello), Florence/SCALA; p47, 3, V&A, 4, Schatzkammer, Munich, p48, Fitzwilliam Museum, Cambridge; p50, V&A; p51, Bayerisches Nationalmuseum, Munich; p52, V&A; p53, V&A; p54, 1, BM, 3, Sotheby's, 2. The Bridgeman Art Library, London; p56: 1, Sotheby's 2, V&A 3. Trustees of the Chatsworth Settlement; p57, BM; p58, box BM, 1. V&A; p59, Diana Scarisbrick; p60, 1 & 2. V&A, 3 BM/Hull Grundy Collection; p61, 1 Danish Royal Collections, Rosenborg Palace, Copenhagen/ Photo Lennart Larsen, 5 & 6, Diamond Information Centre, London/ Walters Art Gallery, Baltimore/Benjamin Zucker Collection; p62, Christie's Geneva; p63, 2. BM, 3. V&A, 4. Museum of London; p64, V&A; p65, box and 4, V&A, 2 & 3 Röhsska Konstslöjdmuseet, Gothenburg; p66, S. J. Phillips; p68, S. J. Phillips, p69, Diana Scarisbrick; p70, V&A; p71, S. J. Phillips; p72, 1. Cabinet des Medailles, 3. V&A, 2. Cabinet des Medailles; p73, 4. Musée des Arts Décoratifs, Bordeaux, 5 & 6, Diana Scarisbrick; p74 Ashmolean Museum, Oxford; p75, 3. Diamond Information Centre, London/Walters Art Gallery, Baltimore/Benjamin Zucker Collection, 4. Ashmolean Museum, Oxford, 5. Ashmolean Museum, 6. Diamond Information Centre, London/Walters Art Gallery, Baltimore/Benjamin Zucker Collection, 7.

Diamond Information Centre, London, 8. Ashmolean Museum; p76, 1. Derek Clifford, 2. BM/Hull Grundy Collection, 3. Private Collection; p77, 4. V&A, 5. BM/Hull Grundy, 6. V&A; p78,1. S. J. Phillips, 2. S. J. Phillips, 3. Derek Clifford, 4. V&A; p79, S. J. Phillips; p80, Private Collection; p81 Box, V&A, 2. S. J. Phillips, 3. David Lavender; p82, V&A; p83, S. J. Phillips; p84, Phillips Fine Art Auctioneers; p86, Phillips Fine Art Auctioneers; p87, Mary Evans Picture Library; p88, Sotheby's; p89 Courtesy of Boucheron, p90, 1, V&A, 2, Silver, London; p91, 3 & 5, The Illustrated London News Picture Library, 4, V&A, 6, Lankesters, Grays Antique Market, London, p92, 1. Phillips Fine Art Auctioneers, 2. Peter Hinks, 3. Sotheby's; p93, 4. BM, 5, 6, Phillips Fine Art Auctioneers, 2. Peter Hinks, 3. Sotheby's; p93, 4. BM, 5, 6, Phillips Fine Art Auctioneers; p94, 1, 2, V&A, 3. Peter Hinks; p95, 4. BM, 5. Sotheby's, box Courtesy of Boucheron; p96, 1. Phillips, 2. Sotheby's, 3. Phillips Fine Art Auctioneers; p97, 5. Phillips Fine Art Auctioneers, 4. Peter Hinks, 6. Phillips Fine Art Auctioneers p98 1. Sotheby's, 2, Peter Hinks, 4. Phillips Fine Art Auctioneers, 3. Sotheby's; p99, 1. Phillips Fine Art Auctioneers; 2. Phillips Fine Art Auctioneers 4. Phillips Fine Art Auctioneers, 3. Peter Hinks; p100, Sotheby's; p101, 6, Phillips Fine Art Auctioneers, 7, Sotheby's, 8, Phillips Fine Art Auctioneers, 9-11 Sotheby's; p102, Phillips Fine Art Auctioneers; p103, 2, Sotheby's, 3-5 Phillips Fine Art Auctioneers, 6 Sotheby's; p104, 1 Sotheby's, 2 Sotheby's; p105, 3, Courtesy of Boucheron, 4-6 Sotheby's; p106, 1 Peter Hinks, 2, Sotheby's, Box National Portrait Gallery, London; p107, Sotheby's; p108, Van den Bosche, Camden Passage, London/photo Eileen Tweedy; p110 Phillips Fine Art Auctioneers; p111, John Jesse & Irina Laski; p112, Tadema Gallery, Camden Passage, London/photo Eileen Tweedy; p113, Tadema Gallery, Camden Passage, London; p114, 1 Noel Tovey/photo Eileen Tweedy, 2-3, Irish Tourist Board, 4, Calouste Gulbenkian Foundation, *Lisbon/© DACS, 1989; p115, 5-6, Sotheby's, 7, Galerie Moderne/© DACS 1989, 8, Virginia Museum of Fine Arts, Richmond, Virginia/Lewis Gift, photo Katherine Wetzel; p116, 1, Tadema Gallery, Camden Passage, London, 2, John Jesse & Irina Laski, 3, Christie's Colour Library; p117, Silver, London, 4, Silver, London, 5, Tadema Gallery, Camden Passage, London, 6, Noel Tovey; p118, 1, Tadema Gallery, Camden Passage, London, 2, The Purple Shop, Antiquarius, London/photo Eileen Tweedy, 3, John Jesse & Irina Laski; p119, 3, Van den Bosche, Camden Passage, London, 4, Tadema Gallery, Camden Passage, London, 5, Virginia Museum of Fine Arts, Richmond, Virginia/Lewis Gift, photo Katherine Wetzel; p120, 1, John Jesse & Irina Laski, 2 Phillips Fine Art Auctioneers; p121, 3 Tadema Gallery, Camden Passage, London, 4, Calouste Gulbenkian Foundation, Lisbon/© DACS 1989, 5, John Jesse & Irina Laski; p122, 1, Tadema Gallery, Camden Passage, London, 2, Christie's Colour Library, 3, Virginia Museum of Fine Arts, Richmond, Virginia/Lewis Gift photo Katherine Wetzel/© DACS 1989; p123, 4, Tadema Gallery, Camden Passage, London, 5, Virginia Museum of Fine Arts, Richmond, Virginia/Lewis Gift photo Katherine Wetzel/© DACS 1989, 6, Tadema Gallery, Camden Passage, London; p124, 1-2, Calouste Gulbenkian Foundation, Lisbon/© DACS 1989, 3, Keith Baker, 4, Macdonald/Aldus Archive; p125, 4, Tadema Gallery, Camden Passage, London, 5, Silver, London, 6, Phillips Fine Art Auctioneers; p126, 1,

Tadema Gallery, Camden Passage, London, 2, Macdonald/Aldus Archive, 3, Tadema Gallery, Camden Passage, London; p127, 4, Van den Bosche, Camden Passage, London, 5-6, Tadema Gallery, Camden Passage, London; p128, Sotheby's; p130, Deirdre O'Day/photo Eileen Tweedy; p131, Nicholas Harris, London; p132, Courtesy of Boucheron; p133, Tadema Gallery, Camden Passage, London; p134, 1, Egyptian State Tourist Office/photo Robbie Jack, 2, Cartier Archive Paris, 3, Musée Cartier, Paris, 4, Angelo Hornak; p135, 5-6 Nicholas Harris, London, 7,© The Colchester Lathe Company Ltd., 8, ET Archive; p136, 1, Alistair Duncan, 2-4, Nicholas Harris, London, 5, Silver, London; p137 Silver, London, 6-8 Nicholas Harris, London; p138, 1, M. Bashir, V27 Antiquarius, London/photo Eileen Tweedy, 2, Sotheby's, 3, Silver, London; p139, 4, La Vérité Ltd, Antiquarius, London/photo Eileen Tweedy, 5, Tadema Gallery, Camden Passage, London, 6, Nicholas Harris, London; p140, 1, Silver, London, 2, Virginia Museum of Fine Arts, Richmond, Virginia/Lewis Gift photo Katherine Wetzel, 3, Nicholas Harris, London; p141, 4, Deirdre O'Day/photo Eileen Tweedy, 5, John Jesse & Irina Laski, 6, Noel Tovey/photo Eileen Tweedy, 7, Silver, London/photo Eileen Tweedy; p142, 1, Michael Hallström, Antiquarius, London/photo Eileen Tweedy, 2, Noel Tovey/photo Eileen Tweedy, 3, Sotheby's; p143, 4, Nicholas Harris, London, 5-6 Noel Tovey/photo Eileen Tweedy, 7, Sotheby's; p114, 1-2 Patricia Bayer/photo Eileen Tweedy, 3, Noel Tovey/photo Eileen Tweedy; p145, 4, Noel Tovey/photo Eileen Tweedy, 5, Patricia Bayer/ photo Eileen Tweedy, 6 Deirdre O'Day, 7 Patricia Bayer/photo Eileen Tweedy; p146 John Jesse; p148, Collection FIFTY-50, New York; p149, John Jesse & Irina Laski; p150, Cartier Archive Paris; p151, John Jesse & Irina Laski; p152-153, 1 BBC Hulton Picture Library, 2, John Jesse & Irina Laski, 3, Noel Tovey/photo Eileen Tweedy, 4, Reproduced by kind permission of the Henry Moore Foundation, 5, The Design Council Picture Library, 6, Tadema Gallery, Camden Passage, London/photo Eileen Tweedy; p154, 1, John Jesse & Irina Laski, 2 & 4, Tadema Gallery, Camden Passage, London/photo Eileen Tweedy, 3, Sotheby's; p155, 5, John Jesse & Irina Laski, 6, Sotheby's, 7, Tadema Gallery, Camden Passage, London/photo Eileen Tweedy; p156, 1, M. Bashir, V27 Antiquarius, London/photo Eileen Tweedy, 2, La Vérité, Antiquarius, London, 3, Tadema Gallery, Camden Passage, London/photo Eileen Tweedy; p157, 4, Patricia Bayer/photo Eileen Tweedy, 5, La Vérité Ltd, Antiquarius, London, 6, Sarah Dwyer & Tony Giorgi, Antiquarius, London; p158, 1, Tadema Gallery, Camden Passage, London/photo Eileen Tweedy, 2, V&A, 3, Collection FIFTY-50, New York; p159, 3, Tadema Gallery, Camden Passage, London/photo Eileen Tweedy, 4, V&A/© COSMOPRESS, GENEVE, DACS, LONDON 1989, 5, V&A; p160, Tadema Gallery, Camden Passage, London/photo Eileen Tweedy; p161, 2-3 Tadema Gallery, Camden Passage, London/photo Eileen Tweedy; p162, William Harper; p164, Friedrich Becker; p165, Barbara Christie/Lesley Craze Gallery, London; p166, Helge Larsen & Darani Lewers; p167, Wendy Ramshaw; p168-169, 1, Donald Judd/Waddington Galleries, London, 2, Herman Hermsen/Galerie Ra, Amsterdam, 3, Remote Source Photographic Library, 4, Lam de Wolfe/Galerie Ra, Amsterdam, 5, Friedrich Becker, 6, V&A; p170, 1, Charles de Temple, 2-3, Tadema Gallery, Camden Passage, London/photo Eileen

Tweedy; p171, Tadema Gallery, Camden Passage, London/photo Eileen Tweedy; p172, Gerda Flöckinger, 1, V&A, 2, Elisabeth Holder; p173, 3, V&A, 4, Catherine Mannheim, 5, Cynthia Cousens; p174, 1, Anne-Marie Shillito, 2, William Harper; p175, 3, Helge Larsen & Darani Lewers, 4, Gijs Bakker/Galerie Ra, Amsterdam/© DACS 1988, 5, Gerd Rothman; p176, 1, Frank Bauer, 2, Joël Degen/Lesley Craze Gallery/photo Joël Degen, 3, V&A, 4, David Watkins, 5, David Poston; p177, Wendy Ramshaw; p178, 1&3, Peter Chang, 2, Katzie Hughes/Lesley Craze Gallery, 4, Geoff Roberts; p179, 5, Clarissa, 6, Monty Don, p180, 1, Onno Boekhoudt/Galerie Ra, Amsterdam, 2, Susanna Heron/photo David Ward, 3, Helge Larsen & Darani Lewers; p181, 4, Peter Tully, 5, Gijs Bakker/Galerie Ra, Amsterdam/© DACS 1989, 6, Otto Kunzli; p182, Charlotte de Syllas/photo Ian Haigh; p183, 2, Richard Mawdsley, 3, Sophie Chell/Courtesy, Worshipful Company of Goldsmiths, 4, Bruno Martinazzi, 5, Viliama Grakalic; p184-185, Robert Ebendorf,

Although we have made every effort to trace and acknowledge all copyright holders, Quarto would like to apologize if there should be any omissions.